Get the eBook FREE!
(PDF, ePub, Kindle, and liveBook all included)

We believe that once you buy a book from us, you should be able to read it in any format we have available. To get electronic versions of this book at no additional cost to you, purchase and then register this book at the Manning website.

Go to https://www.manning.com/freebook and follow the instructions to complete your pBook registration.

That's it!
Thanks from Manning!

The AI Pocket Book

The AI Pocket Book

EMMANUEL MAGGIORI

MANNING
SHELTER ISLAND

For online information and ordering of this and other Manning books, please visit www.manning.com. The publisher offers discounts on this book when ordered in quantity.

For more information, please contact

> Special Sales Department
> Manning Publications Co.
> 20 Baldwin Road
> PO Box 761
> Shelter Island, NY 11964
> Email: orders@manning.com

© 2025 Manning Publications Co. All rights reserved.

No part of this publication may be reproduced, stored in a retrieval system, or transmitted, in any form or by means electronic, mechanical, photocopying, or otherwise, without prior written permission of the publisher.

Many of the designations used by manufacturers and sellers to distinguish their products are claimed as trademarks. Where those designations appear in the book, and Manning Publications was aware of a trademark claim, the designations have been printed in initial caps or all caps.

♻ Recognizing the importance of preserving what has been written, it is Manning's policy to have the books we publish printed on acid-free paper, and we exert our best efforts to that end. Recognizing also our responsibility to conserve the resources of our planet, Manning books are printed on paper that is at least 15 percent recycled and processed without the use of elemental chlorine.

The author and publisher have made every effort to ensure that the information in this book was correct at press time. The author and publisher do not assume and hereby disclaim any liability to any party for any loss, damage, or disruption caused by errors or omissions, whether such errors or omissions result from negligence, accident, or any other cause, or from any usage of the information herein.

Manning Publications Co.	Development editor:	Ian Hough
20 Baldwin Road	Technical editor:	Artur Guja
PO Box 761	Review editor:	Radmila Ercegovac
Shelter Island, NY 11964	Production editor:	Andy Marinkovich
	Copy editor:	Lana Todorovic-Arndt
	Proofreader:	Keri Hales
	Typesetters:	Bojan Stojanović and Tamara Švelić Sabljić
	Cover designer:	Marija Tudor

ISBN 9781633435759
Printed in the United States of America

brief contents

1 ■ How AI works   1
2 ■ Hallucinations   59
3 ■ Selecting and evaluating AI tools   82
4 ■ When to use (and not to use) AI   98
5 ■ How AI will affect jobs and how to stay ahead   117
6 ■ The fine print   146

contents

preface *x*
acknowledgments *xiii*
about this book *xv*
about the author *xviii*
about the cover illustration *xix*

1 How AI works 1

How LLMs work 2

*Text generation 4 ▪ End of text 5 ▪ Chat 5
The system prompt 7 ▪ Calling external software
functions 8 ▪ Retrieval-augmented generation 12*

The concept of tokens 13

*One token at a time 14 ▪ Billed by the token 16
What about languages other than English? 16
Why do LLMs need tokens anyway? 18*

Embeddings: A way to represent meaning 19

*Machine learning and embeddings 20
Visualizing embeddings 21 ▪ Why embeddings
are useful 22 ▪ Why LLMs struggle to analyze
individual letters 23*

CONTENTS vii

The transformer architecture 25

*Step 1: Initial embeddings 28 ▪ Step 2:
Contextualization 29 ▪ Step 3: Predictions 32
Temperature 33 ▪ Can you get an LLM to always
output the same thing? 34 ▪ Where to learn
more 35*

Machine learning 36

*Deep learning 37 ▪ Types of machine learning 38
How LLMs are trained (and tamed) 45 ▪ Loss 47
Stochastic gradient descent 48*

Convolutions (images, video, and audio) 51

Multimodal AI 53

No free lunch 56

2 Hallucinations 59

What are hallucinations? 60

*Made-up facts 60 ▪ Misinterpretation 62
Incorrect solutions to problems 63
Overconfidence 65 ▪ Unpredictability 66*

Why does AI hallucinate? 67

*Inadequate world models 68 ▪ World models:
Theory vs. practice 69 ▪ Misaligned objectives 70
Toy hallucination example: Price optimization 72*

Will hallucinations go away? 74

Mitigation 75

Hallucinations can kill a product 78

Living with hallucinations 80

3 Selecting and evaluating AI tools 82

Proprietary vs. open source 83

How to decide 84

Off-the-shelf vs. fine-tuning 85

How to decide 88

viii CONTENTS

Customer-facing AI apps vs. foundation
models 89

How to decide 89

Model validation, selection, and testing 90

Training set 90 ▪ Validation set 91 ▪ Test set 92

Performance measures 93

*Accuracy 93 ▪ Precision and recall 94 ▪ Mean
absolute error and root mean squared error 96*

4 When to use (and not to use) AI 98

Building an AI-based product 99

*Am I putting AI before the customer? 99
Are hallucinations okay? 102 ▪ Do I need to
explain how the output is generated? 103*

Using conversational AI as an assistant 105

*Can I describe the task succinctly and validate
the output easily? 105 ▪ Has anyone done it
before? 107 ▪ What does an excellent job look
like? 110*

Building LLM wrappers 112

*Will users interact with my product using natural
language? 113*

5 How AI will affect jobs and how to stay ahead 117

Excellence gap 118

*Excellence gap in software engineering 122
Recommendations 124*

Stringent validation 126

*Validation in software engineering 131
Recommendations 133*

CONTENTS

Tight control 136

Control in software 139 ▪ *Recommendations 140*

A new opportunity: Making the web more human 141

Philosophical detour: Automation and mass unemployment 142

6 *The fine print* 146

Copyright 147

Economics of AI 151

Smoke and mirrors 154

Regulation 157

Prohibited AI practices 157 ▪ *High-risk systems 158* ▪ *Transparency obligations 158* *Foundation models 158*

Resource consumption 159

Brains and consciousness 162

appendix A Catalog of generative AI tools 167

index 175

preface

In the 2010s, a methodology known as machine learning became extremely popular. The novelty of machine learning was that, instead of writing every detail of a computer program by hand, some parts were determined automatically by having a computer analyze data. While machine learning wasn't new, it rose to prominence during this period thanks to increased computing power and an unprecedented amount of data ready to be exploited.

Machine learning soon became the favorite methodology of *artificial intelligence,* which is a more general research field that tries to have computers perform tasks similarly to humans. Notably, AI researchers used machine learning to reach record performance in automated analysis of images, video, and text. They also used machine learning to build the famous game-playing software AlphaGo, which beat a human player at the difficult game of Go.

Machine learning also boomed in the business world. For example, companies started using it to automatically analyze online shoppers' data and generate personalized product recommendations.

Due to machine learning's success and wide adoption in the AI field, people soon started using the terms "machine learning" and "AI" interchangeably. The business world became highly enthusiastic about AI's prospects and made big promises. However, while AI expanded steadily in academia and business, it was not massively adopted by the general public. This was probably because general-purpose AI tools weren't all that useful yet (think of Alexa and Siri) and because AI was still not that great at analyzing natural language.

But in the late 2010s and early 2020s, a series of methodological innovations made AI much better at analyzing written language and generating new content. This led to a race to build AI tools that could be used as high-performing assistants by the general public.

AI exploded in 2022, with the launch of a number of remarkable customer-facing AI apps. One of them was ChatGPT, which reached a hundred million users in three months. Another one was Midjourney, a powerful tool for creating realistic images from a textual description.

Enthusiasm about AI soared and so did dramatic predictions about its effects. Some people predicted extreme productivity gains. Others predicted massive unemployment due to AI replacing people's jobs. In particular, many people argued that software engineers would become obsolete.

I'm a software engineer who specializes in AI. I did my PhD in AI and have been involved in the field for over a decade. Early in my career, while I was impressed by AI, I became a bit frustrated by the amount of hype around it—I kept stumbling upon failed AI projects that were swept under the rug, and I had the impression that AI's limitations were often overlooked. In 2023, I published a book on the subject, titled *Smart Until It's Dumb* (Applied Maths Ltd, 2023). As opposed to other books on AI, which were either very positive or negative about it, I wanted to share a more nuanced view. As the title implies, I think AI can be really cool sometimes, but it can be less cool other times—think of those pesky hallucinations that AI often suffers from.

After I wrote that book, people started asking me questions about all things AI related. For example, they asked me whether I thought machines would become conscious or whether self-driving cars would soon roam every street. But the most common topic was the future of work. Specifically, aspiring software engineers seemed particularly concerned about their future careers. People asked me, "Is it even worth becoming a software engineer, now that AI can code?" A teacher told me a few of her students had dropped out because they thought AI would make their skills irrelevant. In addition, numerous software engineers started to use AI at work and build AI-based products, but they often told me they couldn't make it work as intended. For example, they said AI often generated inconsistent outputs, and users didn't appreciate it.

This book is intended to help you ride the AI revolution, both in terms of using AI effectively and making sure your job stays ahead of what AI can do. The book is based on my own experience in the AI field and also on the numerous conversations I've had with people about it. You'll read stories, reflections, and general advice, which I hope you'll find useful.

After you finish the book, I hope you'll feel that you understand AI better, including its limitations, and that you'll discover new ways of using AI effectively and future-proof your career against it.

acknowledgments

The most difficult thing about writing a book is not putting words together or thinking about grammar (which AI is quite good at). Instead, the most difficult thing is writing a book whose content resonates with the target audience.

That's why my biggest thank you goes to the humans who went through this book's draft and shared useful advice to improve it. This includes my developmental editor at Manning, Ian Hough and my technical editor, Artur Guja, risk manager, computer scientist, systems developer, and financial markets professional with over 20 years of experience in the banking sector. I'd also like to thank my acquisitions editor, Andy Waldron, and the wider Manning team who've been extremely helpful throughout the process.

Finally, many thanks to all the reviewers from the software industry who read the draft early on and shared their thoughts: Aarohi Tripathi, Aayush Bhutani, Aeshna Kapoor, Ajay Tanikonda, An Nadein, Anil Kumar Moka, Annie Taylor Chen, Anupam Mehta, Arpankumar Patel, Arpit Chaudhary, Ashish Anil Pawar, Batul Bohara, Devendra Singh Parmar, Divakar Verma, Gajendra Babu Thokala, Harsh Daiya, Karthik Rajashekaran, Lalit Chourey, Maksym Prokhorenko, Manohar Sai Jasti,

Martin Knudsen, Meghana Puvvadi, Mohit Palriwal, Naresh Dulam, Natapong Sornrpom, Nilesh Charankar, Nupur Baghel, Prachit Kurani, Prakash Reddy Putta, Prasann Pradeep Patil, Premkumar Reddy, Raghav Hrishikeshan Mukundan, Radhika Kanubaddhi, Rajeev Reddy Vishaka, Rajesh Daruvuri, Ram Kumar Nimmakayala, Riddhi Shah, Ruchi Agarwal, Sai Chiligireddy, Shivendra Srivastava, Siddharth Parakh, Subba Rao Katragadda, Sudheer Kumar Lagisetty, Sumit Dahiya, Sudharshan Tumkunta, and Vishnu Challagulla. Your feedback helped improve this book.

Thank you all!

about this book

This book will help you navigate the AI revolution, using AI effectively in your work and making sure your job won't be replaced by AI. The book was primarily written for software engineers, but its content was designed to be accessible to other audiences, too. So, there are no prerequisites to read this book, and anyone should be able to understand it. It is helpful, however, to know the basics of coding and math to fully understand all the examples.

The book starts with a plain-English overview of how AI works. It then covers a wide range of timely and controversial AI-related topics such as hallucinations, the future of work, and copyright.

Who should read this book?

Two main groups of people should read this book. The first one is software engineers—aspiring, novice, and seasoned ones—who want to understand the effects of AI on their careers and prepare for it.

The second group includes people related to or interested in the software industry, even if they're not engineers themselves. For example, these are product managers and startup

xvi ABOUT THIS BOOK

entrepreneurs. One of this book's reviewers said he thought the book would be useful not just for software engineers but also for "software sympathizers," which I thought was a good way to put it.

How this book is organized: A road map

The book is divided into six chapters:

- *Chapter 1: How AI works*—This chapter explains how large language models and other types of AI work and how AI is built.

- *Chapter 2: Hallucinations*—This chapter explains the reasons for AI's pesky mistakes (known as hallucinations), whether they will be fixed soon, and what we can do about them.

- *Chapter 3: Selecting and evaluating AI tools*—This chapter explains a method to select and compare different AI tools and avoid common biases in your evaluation.

- *Chapter 4: When to use (and not to use) AI*—This chapter is a checklist that will help you decide whether it is a good idea to use AI to assist you with a certain task or as the building block of a customer-facing product.

- *Chapter 5: How AI will affect jobs and how to stay ahead*—This chapter explains three characteristics of jobs that will help them resist AI advancements and how software engineers can stay relevant in the AI era.

- *Chapter 6: The fine print*—This chapter covers the less flattering side of AI, such as exaggeration, copyright disputes, and dubious comparisons of AI models with the human brain. It is meant to help you get up to speed with some of the bigger questions around AI.

liveBook discussion forum

Purchase of *The AI Pocket Book* includes free access to live-Book, Manning's online reading platform. Using liveBook's exclusive discussion features, you can attach comments to the book globally or to specific sections or paragraphs. It's a snap to make notes for yourself, ask and answer technical questions, and receive help from the author and other users. To access the forum, go to https://livebook.manning.com/book/the-ai-pocketbook/discussion. You can also learn more about Manning's forums and the rules of conduct at https://livebook.manning.com/discussion.

Manning's commitment to our readers is to provide a venue where a meaningful dialogue between individual readers and between readers and the author can take place. It is not a commitment to any specific amount of participation on the part of the author, whose contribution to the forum remains voluntary (and unpaid). We suggest you try asking the author some challenging questions lest their interest stray! The forum and the archives of previous discussions will be accessible from the publisher's website for as long as the book is in print.

about the author

EMMANUEL MAGGIORI, PHD, has been an AI industry insider for 10 years. He has developed AI for various applications, from processing satellite images to packaging deals for holiday travelers. He is the author of the books *Smart Until It's Dumb,* which analyzes the AI industry, and *Siliconned,* which analyzes the wider tech industry.

about the cover illustration

The figure on the cover of *The AI Pocketbook*, captioned "Allay tzaoussou (alay chavushu), ou inspecteur aux parades," or "Allay tzaoussou (alay chavushu), or parade inspector," is from the George Arents Collection, courtesy of the New York Public Library (1808–1826).

In those days, it was easy to identify where people lived and what their trade or station in life was just by their dress. Manning celebrates the inventiveness and initiative of the computer business with book covers based on the rich diversity of regional culture centuries ago, brought back to life by pictures from collections such as this one.

How AI works

This chapter covers

- The way LLMs process inputs and generate outputs
- The transformer architecture that powers LLMs
- Different types of machine learning
- How LLMs and other AI models learn from data
- How convolutional neural networks are used to process different types of media with AI
- Combining different types of data (e.g., producing images from text)

This chapter clarifies how AI works, discussing many foundational AI topics. Since the latest AI boom, many of these topics (e.g., "embeddings" and "temperature") are now widely discussed, not just by AI practitioners but also by businesspeople and the general public. This chapter demystifies them.

Instead of just piling up definitions and writing textbook explanations, this chapter is a bit more opinionated. It points out common AI problems, misconceptions, and limitations

How AI works

based on my experience working in the field, as well as discussing some interesting insights you might not be aware of. For example, we'll discuss why language generation is more expensive in French than in English and how OpenAI hires armies of human workers to manually help train ChatGPT. So, even if you are already familiar with all the topics covered in this chapter, reading it might provide you with a different perspective.

The first part of this chapter is a high-level explanation of how *large language models* (LLMs) such as ChatGPT work. Its sections are ordered to roughly mimic how LLMs themselves turn inputs into outputs one step at a time.

The middle part of this chapter discusses *machine learning*, which is the technique that makes computers learn from data to create LLMs and other types of AI. Note that AI and machine learning don't mean the same. AI is a research field that tries to create computer programs to perform tasks in a way similar to humans. Machine learning may or may not be used for that goal. However, machine learning has been the preferred methodology in AI for at least two decades. So, you might hear people use the terms AI and machine learning interchangeably. When I speak of AI in this book, I mean current AI methods, and these methods involve the use of machine learning.

The last third of this chapter discusses how AI works outside language generation. Specifically, I give an overview of how AI analyzes and generates images or combinations of text and images. We also comment on current developments in AI-based video generation.

Enjoy the ride!

How LLMs work

Language models are computer programs that try to represent the structure of human language. A large language model, or LLM, is a language model on steroids. Its sheer size lets the LLM perform complex analyses of sentences and generate new text with impressive performance. Examples of LLMs are OpenAI's GPT-4o, Meta's Llama-3, Anthropic's Claude 3.5 Sonnet, Google's Gemini 1.5 Pro, and Mistral AI's Mixtral 8x7b.

How LLMs work

Current LLMs are designed to perform one specific task—guess the next word given an input sentence. The input sentence is known as the *prompt*. Suppose I asked you to predict the word that comes after the incomplete sentence "The Eiffel." You're very likely to suggest that "Tower" is the most logical choice. This is the exact job LLMs are designed to do. So, we can think of LLMs as sophisticated autocomplete programs. Officially, we say that LLMs are *autoregressive*, which means that they're designed to produce a single extra piece of content based on previous content.

The autocomplete task may seem simple at first, but it is far-reaching. Consider the following prompt: "How much is 2 + 5? It is. . ." Autocompleting this kind of sentence requires knowing how to perform arithmetic operations. So, the task of performing arithmetic operations is included in the autocomplete task.

Now, consider the following prompt: "How do you say 'umbrella' in French?" To accurately autocomplete this kind of sentence, you'd need to be capable of translating French to English. So, at least in theory, the autocomplete task encompasses all sorts of tasks.

LLMs are created using machine learning, a process in which a computer analyzes a huge amount of data—pretty much a snapshot of the entire public internet—to automatically put the LLM together. The resulting LLM is a self-contained piece of software, meaning that it doesn't access any external information to generate its outputs. For example, it doesn't browse the web to make its next-word predictions. In addition, the LLM is static, so it must be periodically updated with new data if we want it to speak about recent events.

When we interact with LLMs, we don't usually do so directly. Instead, we use an intermediary piece of software that processes our requests and manages the underlying LLM. Let's call it the *LLM wrapper*. The wrapper uses tricks to provide further functionality to the user than just guessing the next word like the bare LLM would do. For example, the wrapper generates entire sentences, responds in a chatty way, and answers with real-time information, such as the current date.

An example of an LLM wrapper is ChatGPT, which is OpenAI's customer-facing application. This application manages our interactions with the underlying LLM, such as GPT-4 and GPT-4o. Note that it is common to just use the term LLM to refer to the whole AI system, including the wrapper.

The next few sections discuss examples of how LLM wrappers use tricks to enhance the capabilities of their underlying, next-word guessing LLMs.

Text generation

We typically use LLMs to output entire sentences instead of just guessing a single word. The LLM wrapper achieves this through a simple trick: it makes the LLM eat its own output repeatedly. Suppose we give an LLM the prompt "The Eiffel." The LLM guesses the most likely continuation of the sentence: "Tower." The LLM wrapper then attaches this word to the initial prompt, which leads to the new prompt: "The Eiffel Tower." It then uses the LLM to guess the following word, say, "is" and attaches it to the prompt again. The process is repeated (see figure 1.1) to generate entire sentences such as "The Eiffel Tower is in Paris."

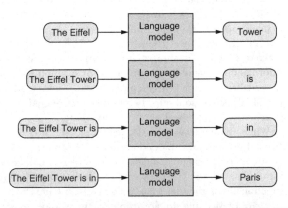

Figure 1.1 To generate full sentences, the LLM wrapper used the LLM to generate one word, then attached that word to the initial prompt, then used the LLM again to generate one more word, and so on.

End of text

In addition to outputting regular words, LLMs are designed to output a handful of special code words. One of them, often stylized as "<|end of text|>" in the literature, is a code word that signals the end of the text. When the LLM is built, it is exposed to examples of sentences containing this special code word to indicate their end. So, the LLM gains the capability of guessing that the next best word is actually an indication of its ending.

When the LLM wrapper encounters this special code word, it stops the process of having the LLM eat its own output to generate more text, as explained in the previous section.

Chat

Have a look at what happened when I inputted the prompt "The Eiffel" to ChatGPT:

 It seems that your sentence was cut off. Were you asking about the Eiffel Tower?

The Eiffel Tower is one of the most iconic landmarks in the world, located in Paris, France. It was designed by Gustave Eiffel and completed in 1889 for the Exposition Universelle, a world's fair held to celebrate the 100th anniversary of the French Revolution. Originally criticized by some of Paris's leading artists and intellectuals for its design, the tower has become a global cultural icon of France and one of the most recognizable structures in the world.

By the looks of it, the LLM is not just autocompleting my input, or else it would have continued with "Tower" instead of telling me that my sentence was cut off.

What happened here was that, behind the scenes, the LLM wrapper inserted a special code word to indicate the end of my prompt. This code word is often stylized as "<|end of prompt|>" in the literature. So, the actual input sent to the LLM by the wrapper was "The Eiffel<|end of prompt|>". During its construction, the underlying LLM was fed examples of dialog ending with "<|end of prompt|>", which is why it recognized that in my sentence, the code word was located at an unusual place.

As we continue chatting back and forth with ChatGPT, the wrapper sends the LLM a history of the entire conversation each time, filled with "<|end of prompt|>" and "<|end of text|>" code words to clearly delimit the beginning and end of each interaction. This helps ChatGPT converse effectively.

OpenAI lets software developers use a more naked version of the LLM wrapper, which doesn't insert the "<|end of prompt|>" code word after the user's prompt. This is available through the API (an API is a way to connect two pieces of software—in this case, your software with OpenAI's software) or the online platform for software developers (see https://platform.openai.com) by using the *completions* mode of the API instead of the default *chat* mode.

> **NOTE** OpenAI's documentation contains a warning sign telling us that the completions mode is "now considered legacy," but it is still available for use as of this writing.

Let's see what happened when I inputted "The Eiffel" to the LLM using the completions mode instead:

Tower was inaugurated on March 31st in 1889. It was originally built as the entrance arch for the 1889 World's Fair, and was only intended to stand for 20 years. However, its unique design and popularity among Parisians and tourists alike led to its preservation and it has become an iconic symbol of France and one of the most recognizable monuments in the world. The idea for the Eiffel Tower came from businessman Gustave Eiffel, who wanted to create a structure that would showcase the advancements in engineering and design during the Industrial Revolution. He and his team spent two years designing and constructing the tower, using over 18,000 individual pieces of wrought iron and 2.5 million rivets.

We can see that the API simply autocompleted my input with a sensible continuation, which is why it started with " Tower" (the word *Tower* with a leading space) instead of telling me that my prompt was incomplete.

The system prompt

I asked, "What is today's date?" The response was

 Today's date is May 30, 2024.

This was the correct response at the time of me asking. This is a bit surprising because, as LLMs simply analyze sentences to guess the next word, they don't have access to real-time data.

What happened here was that ChatGPT secretly inserted additional text before my prompt to provide contextual information to the LLM. This is known as the *system prompt*. We don't know the exact details, but the rumor is that ChatGPT's system prompt is as follows (see https://mng.bz/RVOv):

 You are ChatGPT, a large language model trained by OpenAI. Answer as concisely as possible. Knowledge cutoff: [knowledge cutoff] Current date: [current date and time]

This prompt is secretly inserted every time you start a chat with ChatGPT. Because the date appears in ChatGPT's system prompt, the chatbot can answer questions about the current date, as in the previous example. Note that the knowledge cutoff date is also inserted, which helps ChatGPT inform the user that it cannot answer questions about events that took place after a certain date.

Software developers can interact with OpenAI's LLMs via an API instead of using the customer-facing ChatGPT. The API lets you define what the system prompt is, which is inserted before your initial interactions with the LLM. Figure 1.2 shows a visual interface provided by OpenAI to help developers try out the API. We can see a box dedicated to the system prompt.

I asked the GPT-4o LLM about the current date using OpenAI's API, while leaving the system prompt empty. In figure 1.2, we can see that the LLM refused to answer about the date.

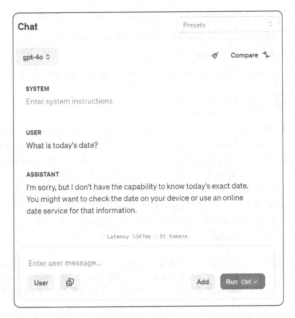

Figure 1.2 OpenAI's API lets users define a system prompt, which is a piece of text inserted into the beginning of the user's prompt.

Figure 1.3 shows that the LLM does answer with the date if it is given as part of the system prompt, like ChatGPT would do.

Calling external software functions

I asked ChatGPT about the current weather in London. ChatGPT's user interface showed a sign that said, "Searching the web." A second later, the sign turned into "Searching current weather in London." Afterward, it told me what the weather in London was like (see figure 1.4).

The trick here is to describe in the system prompt a list of software functions that the LLM can suggest the wrapper to call if it needs to gather external information. If the LLM suggests calling one of those functions, it is the job of the LLM wrapper to call it and then insert the result into the prompt.

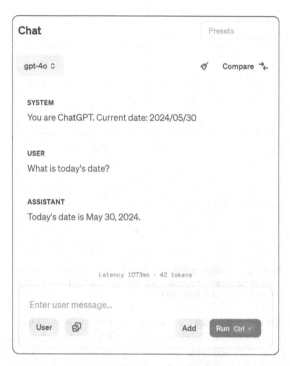

Figure 1.3 When the current date is supplied as part of the system prompt, the LLM can answer questions about the current date.

Suppose a developer wants to create a chatbot app that can seamlessly answer questions about current events, such as the weather, the value of stocks, and trending news topics. The developer could explain in the system prompt that, if the current weather in London is required, the LLM should output "current_weather(London)", if the value of Apple stock is needed, it should output "stock_value(Apple)", and so on. When these special messages are outputted, the developer will call software functions to gather the necessary information and add it to the prompt. This will give the end user the impression of seamless access to real-time data.

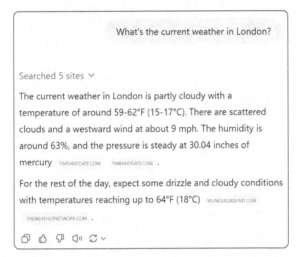

Figure 1.4 ChatGPT called a function to search the web behind the scenes and inserted the results into the user's prompt. This creates the illusion that the LLM browses the web.

OpenAI has created a framework that lets a developer easily define a list of functions that the LLM could suggest calling. Here's an example of how to define a "get_current_weather" function, as described in the official documentation (see https://mng.bz/2y4a):

```
tools = [
    {
        "type": "function",
        "function": {
            "name": "get_current_weather",
            "description": "Get the current weather",
            "parameters": {
                "type": "object",
                "properties": {
                    "location": {
                        "type": "string",
                        "description": "The city and
state,
                            e.g. San Francisco, CA",
```

```
            },
            "format": {
                "type": "string",
                "enum": ["celsius",
"fahrenheit"],
                "description": "The temperature
unit
                to use. Infer this from the
users
                location.",
            },
        },
        "required": ["location", "format"],
    },
    }
  }
]
```

Note that the code of the weather-fetching function is not part of this declaration. Only a description of the function and its inputs is provided. The LLM wrapper inserts the description of this function into the system prompt so that the underlying LLM can suggest calling it if needed.

When the wrapper detects that the LLM suggests calling the function, it notifies the user. Here's an example of the API response object, using OpenAI's Python SDK, that resulted after the user asked about the weather in London:

```
ChatCompletionMessage(
    content=None,
    role='assistant',
    tool_calls=[
    ChatCompletionMessageToolCall(
        id='call_Dn2RJJSxzDm49vlVTehseJ0k',
        function=Function(
            arguments='{"location":"London, United
Kindgdom",
            "format":"celsius"}',
            name='get_current_weather'
        ),
    type='function')
    ]
)
```

The software developer must code the `"get_current_weather"` function, run it, and then insert the response into the following prompt ("Weather in London, United Kingdom: 20 degrees Celsius, rainy"). The LLM can then use this newly added information. The app end user gets the impression that the LLM itself was capable of answering about the weather in real time. In reality, the LLM is still a self-contained program; the enhanced functionality is achieved outside the LLM.

Retrieval-augmented generation

Sometimes users want the LLM to analyze documents that aren't present in the training data. For example, a business may want to answer questions about its internal documents, or an app may want to analyze the content of up-to-date web-pages. Retrieval-augmented generation, or RAG, is a popular way of doing that (you can learn more in *A Simple Guide to Retrieval Augmented Generation* by Abhinav Kimothi, available at https://mng.bz/yWpe). When the user submits a prompt, the LLM wrapper first searches for relevant documents in a database. For example, it may extract keywords from the prompt and find documents that match the keywords. This is known as *retrieval*.

Afterward, the LLM wrapper inserts the content of these documents into the prompt. So, the prompt is said to be *augmented* with additional, relevant information.

When the LLM generates text, it has access to these documents as part of the prompt, so it can use their content to enhance its predictions. RAG is a popular approach to creating an in-house chatbot adapted to a specific business. In addition, it is commonly used to create the illusion that an LLM can access up-to-date web content in real time. RAG can also help identify specific sources used by the LLM to generate its output and thus cite references.

One of the challenges of the RAG approach is finding relevant documents based on the prompt. Many algorithms have been used for a long time by search engines to index and retrieve content, and researchers are studying specific retrieval techniques for RAG (see https://arxiv.org/abs/2405.06211). Another challenge is that prompts can become quite long with the added documents. LLMs only accept a maximum prompt length (more on this in the following), so you must make sure that the documents inserted into the prompt fit the maximum allowed length. In addition, longer prompts incur higher costs as AI providers charge fees that depend on the amount of text inputted and outputted.

The concept of tokens

We've been saying that LLMs guess the next word from an input prompt, but this isn't quite accurate. Let's now refine our understanding.

LLMs contain a fixed-size internal vocabulary. These are the words that LLMs can read and generate. An LLM's vocabulary typically contains

- Common words (e.g., "dog")
- Common pieces of words (e.g., "ish")
- Common Latin characters (e.g., "a" and "b")
- Special symbols from a text-encoding standard called UTF-8, which are combined together to represent non-Latin characters and other symbols (e.g., "á," "æ," and "你")
- Special code words such as "<end of text>" and "<end of prompt>"

Each element in the vocabulary is known as a *token*. We can think of a token as a common piece of text. Using tokens instead of entire words, lets LLMs read and produce words that aren't in the dictionary (e.g., "hungryish") by combining common pieces of words ("hungry" + "ish"). It also lets LLMs read and produce non-Latin text and invent new words.

Current LLMs' vocabularies contain roughly 100,000 different possible tokens. For example, some of OpenAI's LLMs, including GPT-3.5 and GPT-4, have a vocabulary with 100,261 possible tokens.

Note that many tokens represent common words with a leading space attached to them. For example, both "dog" and " dog" are tokens in the vocabulary of OpenAI's LLMs. So, the LLM is often spared from having to use the dedicated whitespace token. From now on, whenever I speak of an individual token in this book, such as the "dog" token, bear in mind there might be a leading space attached to it. (I won't be writing the space every time, as it's a bit ugly to read.)

The vocabulary of an LLM is created by running an automated analysis over thousands of documents to identify the most common text patterns (the algorithm usually used for this is called byte pair encoding. You can find more details and a step-by-step example in a blog article I wrote at https://emaggiori.com/chatgpt-vocabulary/). OpenAI stopped disclosing how it creates LLMs' vocabularies, but we do know how they did it with older models. For example, GPT-3's vocabulary was created by automatically following links from popular Reddit discussions, collecting the text from the linked webpages, and identifying the most common words and combinations of characters in them (Redford et al., "Language Models are Unsupervised Multitask Learners," 2019).

One token at a time

LLMs are designed to read a sequence of valid tokens from their vocabulary. So, the LLM wrapper first subdivides the input prompt into valid tokens. For example, when using GPT-3.5, the prompt "The dog's bark was barely" is subdivided as follows by the LLM wrapper before passing it to the LLM:

```
The| dog|'s| bark| was| barely
```

The subdivision is performed using an algorithm that roughly tries to split the input using the largest possible tokens from the vocabulary.

OpenAI provides a webpage where you can input text and see how it's tokenized before being fed into a model. You can find it at https://platform.openai.com/tokenizer.

LLMs don't read raw text. Instead, the LLM wrapper first converts the input prompt into a list of integers indicating the ID of each token, which is its position in the vocabulary:

```
[791, 5679, 596, 54842, 574, 20025]
```

Afterward, the wrapper uses the LLM to predict the ID of the most likely next token. In the previous example, the LLM outputs that the token with ID 80415 is the most likely continuation of the input prompt. This token corresponds to "audible". The LLM wrapper then attaches that token to the input:

```
The| dog|'s| bark| was| barely| audible
```

Next, the LLM wrapper feeds this new prompt (as a list of integers, [791, 5679, 596, 54842, 574, 20025, 80415]) to the LLM to have it "eat its own output" and generate one more token. This process is repeated many times to generate more tokens:

```
The| dog|'s| bark| was| barely| audible| above| the|
roar| of| the| city| traffic|.
```

In this example, after a few more paragraphs of mumbo jumbo regarding dogs and noise, the LLM decided that the token with ID 100276 was the most likely continuation of the prompt. This token is code for "<|end of text|>". So, the LLM deemed this a good place to end the text. Upon stumbling on this token, the LLM wrapper heeded the LLM's recommendation and stopped generating more text.

Have a look at how GPT-3.5 explained to me the meaning of the word "hungryish", token by token:

```
If| you| say| "|I|'m | hungry|ish|,"| you| mean|
you|'re | feeling| somewhat| hungry|,| but| not|
extremely| so|.| It|'s | a| mild|er| form| of| hunger|.
```

We can see that, even though the word "hungryish" isn't part of GPT-3.5's vocabulary, it managed to generate it using a sequence of two tokens, "hungry" and "ish." Note that the words "milder," "I'm," "you're," and "It's" were also produced using two tokens each.

Billed by the token

Most LLM APIs, which let software developers use LLMs programmatically, bill users by the number of tokens inputted and outputted to the LLM. Thus, longer prompts and longer responses incur higher costs.

As of today, for example, GPT-4o costs US$5 per million input tokens plus US$15 per million output tokens. For reference, the entire Shakespearean play *Romeo and Juliet* requires 40,000 tokens, so inputting it to GPT-4o would cost $0.20, and generating it would cost $0.60. This doesn't sound like a lot, but bills can easily add up if you use LLMs repeatedly. For example, if you send a long prompt to an LLM every time a user visits your website, you could spend thousands a month.

Note that when you chat back and forth with an LLM, you must include your entire chat history on every interaction with it, or at least you must do so if you want the LLM to be able to analyze the previous conversation when generating new outputs. So, the prompt becomes increasingly expensive as your chat history becomes longer.

What about languages other than English?

LLM's vocabularies tend to be optimized for the English language. For example, they contain a "dog" token but not one to represent the French word for dog. So, words not in English tend to be split into many tokens, often covering one or two letters at a time, as the vocabulary doesn't contain as many tokens to represent entire words.

Have a look at how the preamble of the U.S. Constitution is tokenized before being inputted into GPT-4:

```
We| the| People| of| the| United| States|,| in| Order|
to| form| a| more| perfect| Union|,| establish|
Justice|,| insure| domestic| Tran|qu|ility|,| provide|
for| the| common| defense|,| promote| the| general|
Welfare|,| and| secure| the| Bless|ings| of| Liberty|
```

The concept of tokens

17

```
to| ourselves| and| our| Poster|ity|,| do| ord|ain|
and| establish| this| Constitution| for| the| United|
States| of| America|.
```

And now, have a look at its French translation:

```
Nous|,| le| Pe|uple| des| É|t|ats|-Un|is|,| en| vue|
de| former| une| Union| plus| par|fa|ite|,| d|'é
|tabl|ir| la| justice|,| de| faire| rég|ner| la|
pa|ix| int|érie|ure|,| de| pour|voir| à| la| déf|ense|
commune|,| de| dévelop|per| le| bien|-être| général|
et| d|' |ass|urer| les| bien|fa|its| de| la| libert|é|
à| nous|-m|ê|mes| et| à| notre| post|é|rit|é|,| nous|
dé|cr|é|tons| et| é|tab|lis|sons| cette| Constitution|
pour| les| É|t|ats|-Un|is| d|' |Am|érique|.
```

The French text takes more than twice the number of tokens than its English counterpart. In addition, the subdivision of words in French doesn't make much sense. For example, "États-Unis d'Amérique" (United States of America) is chopped up into many meaningless pieces such as "ats" and "-Un."

This problem gets even more serious with non-Latin alphabets. An extreme example, widely discussed around the internet, is the word for "woman" in Telugu, one of the languages spoken in India: ꀨ. This word is made up of a combination of six characters arranged horizontally and vertically. GPT-4 requires a whopping 18 tokens to represent this word using special UTF-8 tokens.

As LLMs are billed by the token, the higher number of tokens can make them more expensive to use in other languages compared to English. In addition, it can be more challenging for the LLM to analyze the prompt because individual inputs, such as an "é" token, don't carry much meaning by themselves; the LLM must work extra hard to contextualize adjacent tokens and derive meaning from them.

The bias toward a specific language—English in the most popular LLMs—may not be easily removed. To better tokenize words in other languages, the vocabulary would have to be extended to include words or common pieces of words in, say,

French, Chinese, Telugu, and so on. This would multiply the vocabulary size, well beyond the current 100,000 mark, which could turn LLMs ineffective and slow.

OpenAI has been working on improving its LLMs' internal vocabularies to better handle non-English text. The details haven't been disclosed yet as of this writing, but its creators shared a few illustrative cases with the new vocabulary used by GPT-4o (see https://openai.com/index/hello-gpt-4o/). For example, a snippet of text in Telugu requires 3.5× fewer tokens than before, but it still requires twice as many as its English counterpart.

Why do LLMs need tokens anyway?

One may wonder why tokens are needed at all; that is, why not have the LLM directly read and generate individual characters instead? As we'll discuss soon, LLMs try to internally describe the *meaning* of each individual input. Describing the meaning of a token such as "Paris" is quite easy. For instance, we could describe it as "capital of France." However, describing the meaning of a token such as "P" is much harder, as we don't know what the letter refers to unless we analyze the context. That's why it's much more straightforward to take "Paris" as a single token in one go. The same goes for generating text—it's much more straightforward to let the LLM output a token such as "Paris," which carries a strong meaning by itself, instead of having it output the same word one character at a time.

We could take this idea to the extreme and create a huge vocabulary that includes all sorts of words and their derivatives, such as "Parisian," "Parisians," "Parisian weather," and "Emily in Paris." But this would go too far—the vocabulary would become huge, and it would be wasteful because many tokens would represent closely related ideas. The current setup, with tokens representing the most common words and pieces of words, is an in-between solution that works well in practice.

Embeddings: A way to represent meaning

One of the greatest challenges of AI is finding an effective way to represent high-level concepts, meaning, and ideas. When designing an LLM, we want the model to internally represent the meaning of a token instead of its letters. For example, we want the token "dog" to be represented by a description of what a dog is (say, a friendly, four-legged animal).

An *embedding* is one of the most common ways of representing meaning. It is used by LLMs and other types of AI. An embedding is a list (or "vector") of numbers. The number of elements in the vector is known as the embedding's *dimension*.

We can think of each position in this vector as a measure of how much a token matches a certain topic. Let's have a look at an example. Imagine an embedding vector of length five represents the following five topics: "Animal," "Cat," "Large," "Scary," and "Four legs." Suppose we want to represent the meaning of the "dog" token using these topics. Figure 1.5 provides an (imagined) solution.

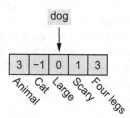

Figure 1.5 Each token is mapped to a vector of numbers. We can imagine that each number in the vector represents a topic. Here's an imaginary list of topics and their respective numbers for the "dog" token.

In this illustration, the token was mapped to five numbers, each of them indicating how much the meaning of the token matches each topic. We can see that the token scores a high value with respect to the "Animal" topic, as a dog is certainly an animal. The token scores a negative value with respect to the "Cat" topic, as a dog is sometimes seen as the opposite of a cat. It scores a neutral value of zero with respect to "Large" because we don't typically think of a dog as being a particularly large or small object. Figure 1.6 shows how we could imagine the embedding for the "elephant" token.

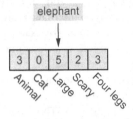

Figure 1.6 An imaginary embedding vector for the "elephant" token

In this case, the embedding vector is neutral with respect to "Cat" and highly positive with respect to "Large."

LLMs are all about embeddings. LLMs go to great lengths to try to find a good, contextualized representation of tokens by using embeddings. At the end of many layers of processing, the embeddings are very good at representing the true meaning of the input tokens, which makes it easy for the LLM to do the job of guessing the next token.

LLMs use much longer embedding vectors than in the above example, which lets them represent a huge number of topics. For example, GPT-3 uses 12,288-dimensional embeddings, so each input token is represented by 12,288 numbers. The smallest model in the Llama 3 family, developed by Meta, uses embeddings of 4,096 dimensions, and the largest one uses embeddings of 16,384 dimensions (https://arxiv.org/abs/2407.21783).

Machine learning and embeddings

Designing long embeddings by hand would be very difficult. Thus, we use *machine learning* to do the job instead. This means that we make a computer analyze a large amount of data, such as text collected from the internet, to come up with useful embeddings.

When AI engineers use, say, 12,288-dimensional embeddings inside an LLM, what they do is leave room for 12,288 topics. However, it is up to the machine to select and organize the topics to best attain its objectives.

As embeddings are created automatically, it is very hard to know which topics are represented by each of their dimensions. In addition, the topics may not be as clear-cut as "Large" and "Cat." So, by using machine learning, we can create effective embeddings—the proof being that LLMs work well—but we can't understand exactly how they work. *Explainability* is sacrificed in the name of predictive power.

Visualizing embeddings

A location on Earth can be determined by its latitude and longitude. We can equally think of each number inside an embedding vector as coordinates that help us figure out where the token is inside a space of meaning. Figure 1.7 illustrates an example of the space of meaning defined by a 2D embedding vector with the topics "Scary" and "Large." Every token is placed inside this space according to its "Scary" and "Large" values in the embedding vector.

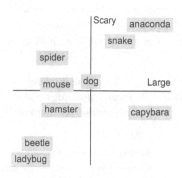

Figure 1.7 We can think the numbers in an embedding vector as coordinates that place the token in a multidimensional "meaning space."

You can see that similar objects tend to group together; that's why the tokens "anaconda" and "snake" are close together in this space and so are "beetle" and "ladybug," but "anaconda" and "ladybug" are far apart.

Well-designed, useful embeddings are such that tokens that are closely related in terms of meaning are also placed close together within this imaginary embedding space. If embedding vectors do a bad job at representing the true meaning of tokens, then related tokens will not be close together in this imaginary embedding space.

As embedding vectors are usually very long, the embedding space is high-dimensional. We can't draw it, but we can still imagine that, in this high-dimensional space, related tokens are physically clustered together.

Why embeddings are useful

Embedding vectors are particularly useful because it's possible to compare them or extract information from them very easily, just by performing simple, linear calculations. Suppose you want to compare the meaning of two tokens. You can do that by calculating their physical distance in the imaginary embedding space. One popular way of doing that is calculating the *dot product* between the two vectors, which produces a sort of "signed distance" between them. If the result is positive, the tokens are close enough in the embedding space and thus their meanings are related. If it's zero, they are unrelated. If it's negative, their meanings are opposed, such as in "large" and "small."

> **NOTE** The dot product is calculated by multiplying the numbers in one vector by their corresponding numbers in the other vector (at the same position) and then adding the results.

Now, suppose you want to extract a limited amount of information of interest from a much more expressive embedding vector. For example, you may want to extract animal-related topics and dump everything else. We can think of this as squashing the multidimensional embedding space into a lower-dimensional space, such as flattening the 3D space to turn it into a thin plate, thus discarding uninformative dimensions. We could imagine, for instance, squashing the entire 12,288-dimensional space into, say, a 100-dimentional space that only focuses on animal-related topics (e.g., "Barks," "Mammal," "Pet"). The mathematical operation to perform such a squashing is known as a *projection*.

A projection is performed by multiplying a matrix by the embedding vector. The matrix represents the direction in which we want to squeeze the embedding space. Note that, as we don't usually understand how embeddings encode meaning, we don't understand how meaning is represented in the squeezed embedding space. Just like with the embeddings, the projections into squeezed spaces are also determined through machine learning and not designed by hand.

In addition to their use within LLMs and other types of AI, it has become popular for engineers to use third-party tools to generate embeddings for all sorts of content-retrieval applications. For example, you can use an embeddings API to generate embeddings that represent the meaning of text documents, and then you compare documents by calculating the dot product of their embeddings. Specifically, OpenAI provides an embeddings API that helps generate an embedding for a text document.

In addition, some APIs generate embeddings for different input modalities, such as text and images. One example is Google Clouds' embeddings API (see https://mng.bz/1Xvq). The generated embeddings can be directly compared. For example, a piece of text speaking about cats and a picture of a cat are mapped to closely related embedding vectors. Thus, you can use dot products to find the image that best matches a description.

Why LLMs struggle to analyze individual letters

LLMs are notorious for struggling to correctly analyze the individual letters in words, such as counting the number of occurrences of a letter. They also struggle to follow instructions that require generating text with certain letters in it. Figure 1.8 shows an example of this problem using GPT-4o.

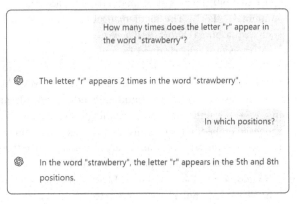

Figure 1.8 **LLMs often struggle to analyze individual letters in words.**

If you remember, LLMs receive tokens as inputs, not letters. So, the exact letters of a word are not inputted to the model. In the example of figure 1.8, the token "berry" is inputted to the LLM in one go.

Each token is then mapped to an embedding vector to represent its meaning. So, any references to individual letters are likely to be completely lost at this stage, as it'd be wasteful to devote space in the embedding vector to represent topics such as "token with two times the letter a," when there are much more useful topics to represent instead.

As people have been widely mocking LLMs' terrible performance at analyzing letters, it's likely AI engineers will take ad hoc measures to directly address this problem. For example, the LLM wrapper may augment the prompt with words' spellings if it detects that there are questions about individual letters. Maybe some of this has already been done, as newer LLMs seem to struggle less to analyze individual letters. However, the problem persists in even the most recent LLMs as of this writing, so it hasn't been fully solved yet.

The transformer architecture

The methodology that powers current LLMs was invented by a group of Google researchers. It was described in a famous paper, published in 2017, titled "Attention Is All You Need" (available at https://arxiv.org/abs/1706.03762). The paper proposed a new way of designing language models, which became known as the *transformer architecture* or just *transformers*.

If you remember, when I asked an LLM to complete the sentence "the dog's bark was barely," it correctly outputted "audible." Despite its apparent simplicity, this sentence is challenging because the word "bark" has two distinct meanings—the noise made by a dog and the coating of a tree. If I asked an LLM to continue the sentence "the tree's bark was barely," then "audible" would be a poor choice. I tried it, and the LLM outputted "visible" instead of "audible." The LLM managed to correctly disambiguate the word "bark" based on whether "dog" or "tree" appeared earlier in the sentence. The transformer architecture was especially designed to effectively disambiguate tokens based on their context.

Before the transformer architecture, the most popular language models were based on a type of AI model known as LSTM (long short-term memory). LSTMs try to predict the next token based on the following two things:

- The last token in the input prompt ("barely" if the input is "the dog's bark was barely")
- A single embedding that summarizes the meaning of all the previous tokens (a single embedding vector that represents "the dog's bark was")

These two pieces of information are used to predict the next token ("audible" in this case). As the entire context before the last token is squashed into a single, fixed-sized embedding vector, LSTMs can process inputs of varying lengths without any complications. This is one of the reasons they became so popular. But this is also LSTMs' Achilles' heel—by squashing such a large context into a single vector, they often lose important, fine-grained contextual information necessary to properly guess the next word.

The transformer architecture solved this problem by processing the previous tokens in a different way, without squashing them all. The process, which follows three steps, is depicted in figure 1.9.

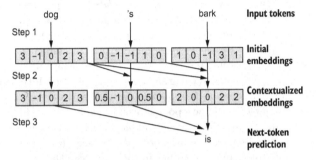

Figure 1.9 LLM overview. In step 1, the tokens are mapped to embeddings one by one. In step 2, each embedding is improved by contextualizing it using the previous tokens in the prompt. In step 3, the much-improved embeddings are used to make predictions about the next token.

First, the model maps each token in the input prompt to an embedding vector that seeks to represent its meaning. This is performed on each token separately, so no contextual information is used—each token is processed as if the other ones didn't exist. While these embeddings can be okay sometimes, they can't be too good because in many cases, it's hard to know the true meaning of a token without looking at the context. For example, the embedding generated for a token such as "bark" will be poor because the model can't know if it refers to dogs or trees.

In the second step, the LLM improves the embedding of each individual token by analyzing its previous tokens—each token is *transformed* by taking its context into account. Note that, compared to LSTMs, the transformer architecture does

The LLM uses a fixed number of previous tokens to contextualize each token, which is known as the *context window*. For example, suppose an LLM has a context window of 10,000 tokens. Each token is contextualized by analyzing its previous 9,999 tokens. If the user's prompt is shorter than 10,000 tokens, then the beginning of the prompt is padded with dummy values like zeros until it reaches 10,000 tokens. If the user's prompt is longer than 10,000 tokens, then the LLM wrapper rejects the user request or drops the beginning of the prompt.

You need to carefully consider the context window before using an LLM. If you want to, say, ask an LLM to summarize an entire novel, you need to make sure that it fits within the context window, or the LLM won't be able to summarize the entire novel at once. In addition, if you use a RAG approach to insert the content of relevant documents into a user's prompt, you also need to make sure the context window can fit them all. Moreover, when you chat back and forth with an LLM-based app, the entire history of the conversation is usually included in each prompt, making the prompt longer as you converse with the chatbot.

Earlier LLMs had very limited context windows. For example, GPT-3's context window was 2,048 tokens. Therefore, their capabilities to analyze long inputs were limited.

Over time, the context window has grown. As of this writing, OpenAI's latest model, GPT-4o, has a context window of 128,000 tokens. And one of Google's models, Gemini 1.5 Pro, offers a context window of 1 million tokens to its enterprise customers. The size of the context window is specified in an LLM's official documentation.

After the end of this contextualization step, the embeddings associated with each input token are much more accurate and thus useful than the initial ones, thanks to contextualization. For example, we could imagine that the embedding for "bark" becomes more animal-like at the end of step 2 if the word "dog" appears before. Conversely, its embedding would become more tree-like if the context contains tree references.

The third step in the transformer architecture (see figure 1.9) is to predict the next token based on the enhanced, contextualized embeddings generated in step 2. This is performed through a very simple mathematical operation because it is assumed that step 2 produced really good embeddings that can help guess the next word very easily.

In the next few sections, we describe each of the three steps in more detail, and we explain how machine learning enters the picture.

Step 1: Initial embeddings

The initial embeddings are obtained very easily. The LLM contains an internal dictionary that maps each possible token to its corresponding embedding. We could imagine it as follows:

```
"a"         -> [0, -1, 2, 3, 1, …]
"b"         -> [1, -2, 0, 4, 0, …]
…
" bark"     -> [1, 0, -1, 3, 1, …]
…
" dog"      -> [3, -1, 0, 2, 3, …]
…
```

The initial embeddings are created by looking up each token in the dictionary and replacing it with its corresponding embedding. The result is an initial set of embeddings, created one by one without context, which concludes step 1 (see figure 1.9).

The numbers inside the dictionary are not defined by hand. These numbers are all *learnable parameters* of the model. This means that the AI engineer leaves them as blanks in the code and lets the computer fill in their values later, when the learning algorithm runs. We can think of the previous dictionary as follows from the point of view of the AI engineer:

```
"a"      -> [?, ?, ?, ?, ?, …]
"b"      -> [?, ?, ?, ?, ?, …]
…
```

```
"bark"      -> [?, ?, ?, ?, ?, …]
…
"dog"       -> [?, ?, ?, ?, ?, …]
…
```

When the computer fills in the blanks, which is known as *learning* or *training*, it designs its own embedding space. So, the computer is free to organize tokens and pick topics as it wishes to attain its goal of effectively guessing the next word.

Consider a model whose vocabulary contains 100,000 different tokens and whose embeddings contain 10,000 dimensions, as is the case with many LLMs. The dictionary would contain 100,000 entries, and each entry would contain 10,000 numbers, which are question marks. The total number of learnable parameters (the question marks) would be $100,000 \times 10,000 =$ 1 billion. That's a lot of learnable parameters! And it's just the beginning.

Step 2: Contextualization

In the second step, the LLM contextualizes each of the input tokens, one by one, by considering its previous tokens (within the context window). Let's see, for example, how the LLM would contextualize the token "bark" in "dog's bark".

Contextualization starts by calculating an attention score for each token in the context. The attention score indicates how it's best to divide attention among all the tokens in the context window to disambiguate the last one. For example, to contextualize "bark", it's worth focusing most of your attention on "dog," followed by "bark" itself, and finally by "'s". Figure 1.10 represents this operation.

The calculation of attention scores, known as the *attention mechanism*, is performed through a series of mathematical operations, such as projections on the embedding vectors (see section 1.3.3). We won't cover the details here, so let's just say that these operations are specially designed to let the LLM extract meaning from the embeddings and compare them.

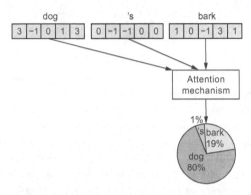

Figure 1.10 The attention mechanism calculates the relative relevance of all tokens in the context window to contextualize or disambiguate the last token.

The AI engineer determines the type of number of operations but leaves blanks that are determined later using machine learning. For example, the numbers inside projection matrixes, which configure what projections do, are left as blanks. Thus, we can picture a projection matrix as

$$[[???...?],$$
$$[???...?],$$
$$...$$
$$[???...?]]$$

So, the AI engineer tells the computer how to disambiguate tokens—by using projections to compare embeddings, and so on—but lets the machine fill in the details. The machine discovers by itself useful ways of analyzing the embeddings to disambiguate problematic tokens like "bark". Projection matrices are rather large, so this step can easily add a few hundred million, if not billions of learnable parameters to the model.

Once the LLM has calculated attention scores, it uses the resulting values to guide the contextualization of tokens' embedding vectors. We can think of this step as letting information from tokens rub off onto other tokens using the attention score for guidance.

For example, a lot of information from "dog" rubs off on "bark", as its attention mechanism determined that the token "dog" was relevant to the meaning of "bark". As a consequence of this step, the embedding for "bark" becomes more animal-like, as opposed to tree-like. Conversely, very little information from "'s" rubs off on "bark", as the attention score deems it rather irrelevant. The process of updating the embeddings based on the context is known as the *feed-forward* step of the transformer.

In the previous example, the end result of the attention and feed-forward mechanisms is an improved version of the embedding for "bark". The same process is applied to contextualize all the tokens in input the prompt, using their previous ones, which leads to a new generation of improved embeddings, as illustrated in step 2 of figure 1.9.

At the end of this process, the LLM is in a much better position to make a guess about the next token, as it contains an improved, contextualized representation of the meaning of the entire input prompt.

MULTILAYER ARCHITECTURE

The contextualization step we just described (step 2) is usually applied multiple times. So, the embedding vectors are improved many times. This is known as a *multilayer* transformer. Most LLMs contain at least a few tens of layers of transformers applied in sequence. Each transformer layer has its own set of learnable parameters, so each layer can specialize in different contextualization tasks.

GPT-3, for example, has 96 transformer layers. This leads to a whopping total of 175 billion learnable parameters inside the model.

MULTIHEADED ATTENTION

The attention mechanism is often subdivided into different heads, meaning that it analyzes different parts of the embedding vectors separately, one chunk at a time. This forces the LLM to design embedding vectors with highly specialized segments. For example, we could imagine that one segment is dedicated to all things animal related and another one to all things tree related, although we still can't usually understand the embedding vectors. This has been observed to work better in practice than having a single head that processes the entire embedding vector at once.

Step 3: Predictions

The last step, step 3 in figure 1.9, is to make a prediction about the most likely next token, which is the LLM's ultimate job. This is performed through projections over the contextualized embeddings generated in step 2.

While we've been saying that LLMs predict the most likely next token, that's not quite accurate. In reality, they calculate a probability value for each possible token in the vocabulary. So, the LLM's output is a vector with as many numbers as tokens in the vocabulary. Each position refers to one possible token, as shown in table 1.1. In this example, the token "audible" receives a high probability of 0.8, meaning that the LLM deems it a highly likely next token.

Table 1.1   In the last step, the LLM assigns a probability value for each possible token in the vocabulary. All the values add to 1.

0.01	0.0	0.05	...	0.8	...
"a"	"b"	"c"		"audible"	

The LLM wrapper picks the next token based on the LLM's output probabilities. One way to do this is to pick the token with the highest probability according to the LLM (in the unlikely event that two tokens have the exact same probability, either one can be picked at random). However, there are other ways to do this, which lets the LLM get more adventurous. We will discuss this next.

Temperature

As discussed in the previous section, LLMs output a probability for each token that describes how likely it is to come right after the input prompt. One way to select the next token from the vocabulary is to pick the one with the highest probability according to the LLM. However, this encourages the LLM to play it a bit too safe—sometimes we want a more adventurous output. So, instead, the next token is often selected by randomly *sampling* a token from the vocabulary using the LLM's output probabilities. For example, if the LLM outputs a probability of 0.9 for the "audible" token, then the sampler picks that token with 90% probability and other ones with 10% probability.

The user can usually regulate how adventurous the output should be by adjusting a setting known as the *temperature*. This setting squeezes or smooths out the LLM's output probabilities. A low temperature pushes the highest sampling probabilities upward and lowers the others. For example, a probability of 0.9 may be transformed into 0.95, while a probability of 0.05 may be transformed into 0.01. This makes it more likely for the LLM wrapper to pick tokens at the top of the ranking. We can think of this as making the LLM wrapper more conservative, as it becomes more prone to select the most obvious tokens at the top of the ranking and less prone to pick alternative ones.

Conversely, a high temperature smooths out probabilities. For example, a probability of 0.9 may be transformed to 0.8, and a probability of 0.01 may be transformed to 0.05. This makes the output more creative by making lower-ranked tokens more likely to be picked. Each LLM wrapper offers its own range of temperature values. OpenAI's API, for example, allows users to set the temperature to a value between zero (conservative) and two (creative).

In the following paragraphs, we describe two alternative ways of setting how adventurous we want our output to be.

Top-p

An alternative setting known as *Top-p* is a cutoff level of cumulative probability. If we set Top-p to, say, 0.8, then we only sample from the top tokens that cover 80% of the probability. The tokens covering the bottom 20% of probability are ignored.

Top k

The *Top-k* setting imposes a limit on the number of top tokens we can sample from. For example, if we set Top-k to 20, the LLM wrapper is only allowed to pick a token among the top-20 tokens. If we set Top-k to 1, we force the LLM to pick the top token every time.

Note that not all LLM wrappers let users configure all these settings—sometimes only one or two of them are available. For example, as of today, OpenAI lets users set temperature and Top-p but not Top-k. The available settings are described in the documentation.

Can you get an LLM to always output the same thing?

It is sometimes desirable to generate *reproducible* outputs with an LLM, meaning that the LLM generates the exact same output every time it's given the same input prompt. This can be useful to benchmark the performance of LLMs or share examples of LLMs' outputs that others can replicate.

It is theoretically possible to have an LLM generate reproducible outputs. For example, this could be achieved by using a top-1 sampling strategy, in which we always pick the token with the highest probability, thus making sure that all mathematical calculations inside the LLM are performed exactly the same way on different runs.

However, while this is theoretically possible, it is not always the case in practice. As of today, for example, it's not possible to guarantee that OpenAI's LLMs will generate the exact same output on different runs. There is official guidance on how to configure settings to produce mostly reproducible outputs, but they're not guaranteed to be exactly alike (see https://mng .bz/PdeR).

This probably happens because popular AI and arithmetic libraries divide a calculation into multiple threads which can be executed in different orders every time (see https://news .ycombinator.com/item?id=37006224). This can cause slight differences in outputs due to round-off errors when adding the same numbers in different orders (see https://mng.bz/JYQZ). In the future, if these problems are fixed, it will be possible to generate reproducible outputs with popular LLM APIs.

Where to learn more

In this section, we've covered the gist of how LLMs work. We haven't discussed the implementation details, such as the exact calculations performed inside the LLM, but we did discuss the overall process LLMs follow to make their predictions.

If you want to know the details, I recommend you to directly have a look at the publicly available source code of GPT-2 (https://mng.bz/wJR5). The file called models.py is the most important one; it defines the entire model in a very compact way (just 174 lines). The code is moderately easy to follow if you understand some Python coding and the TensorFlow library and start from the bottom of the file. I also recommend you read a guide called *The Illustrated Transformer* (https://mng.bz/ qxlx) to learn the details of the architecture.

Even if you don't want to go through all the code, a quick skim through it reveals that the LLM is genuinely just a sequence of simple mathematical operations. As you can see in the code, each layer (called a "block") first calculates the attention scores ("attn") and then uses them to update the embeddings ("mlp"). Projections ("matmul") are among the most common operations performed by the model.

We've now covered how LLMs generate their predictions and mentioned that their details are filled in using machine learning. We haven't, however, described how learning unfolds. That's where we move next.

Machine learning

In traditional software development, the engineer writes every single line of code to tell the computer exactly what to do. Machine learning, or ML, is a different way of creating programs (these programs are known as *models* in ML jargon).

The ML approach comprises two steps. The first step is designing the *architecture* of the solution, which in ML means a template of the steps the program will follow to accomplish the task. Have a look at a piece of Python code using the popular ML library PyTorch:

```
import torch
embedding = torch.nn.Embedding(num_embeddings=100000,
embedding_dim=10000)
projection = torch.nn.Linear(10000, 2000)
model = torch.nn.Sequential(embedding, projection)
```

In the first line, the engineer defines an embedding operation that maps a vocabulary of 100,000 tokens to embedding vectors of length 10,000, similar to what LLMs do. In the second line, the engineer defines a projection to transform an embedding vector of length 10,000 into one of length 2,000. The third line applies each of those operations sequentially, first the embedding and then the projection.

We can see that the engineer puts together the building blocks of the model manually. However, the model has blanks in it, known as *parameters*, which are not defined by hand. In the above example, the embedding block contains 1 billion parameters ($100{,}000 \times 10{,}000$) which are not defined by hand. The second building block, the projection, contains over 20 million parameters (I'll leave the math to you).

Note that the architecture of a machine learning model is designed carefully—the building blocks are introduced with a specific intention in mind and in a way that is tailor-made to the application. For example, the transformer architecture is designed to contextualize words.

The following step in the ML approach is known as *training* or *learning*. The choice between these two words is down to

Machine learning

grammar—you typically say that a person trains a model and that the machine learns.

During training, the engineer runs an algorithm that tries to find the best way of setting the model's parameters (filling in the blanks in the template) to accomplish the desired task. The training algorithm uses data for guidance—usually lots of it—to find promising ways of adjusting the parameter values to improve the model's performance.

The training step is time-consuming and data-hungry, but, if all goes well, the resulting model is often seen to perform much better than if we tried to write the entire program by hand. This is mainly due to the following reasons:

- The process is data-driven, so we rely on evidence to build the best model instead of intuition.
- The model can be millions of times larger than a manually written program.
- The training process can identify serendipitous ways of solving the problem that engineers wouldn't rely on if writing the program manually.

Throughout this section, we'll dig a bit deeper into how machine learning works and discuss common terminology.

Deep learning

In earlier machine learning, the engineer would first write a dedicated piece of software to extract representative *features* from the input. For example, the engineer would write a dedicated algorithm to extract keywords from text or detect lines in an image. Afterward, a small ML model would be used to make predictions from these manually engineered features. This process can be summarized as follows:

Raw input -> Feature engineering -> Model -> Prediction

In deep learning, which is a type of machine learning, the model processes much rawer inputs, such as tokens or an unprocessed input image:

How AI works

Raw input -> Model -> Prediction

In deep learning, the model itself learns a useful way to represent the input—it performs its own feature engineering. We saw that in action with LLMs: the machine works hard to produce contextualized embeddings to represent the meaning of the input tokens. To process rawer inputs, the model usually contains multiple layers of processing stacked on top of each other, which is where the name "deep" comes from.

In many applications within text generation and image analysis, deep learning is much more accurate than the previous two-step process with manually engineered features. This requires, however, devising an effective architecture for the task, such as the transformer architecture.

Note that there's still a place for old-school, "shallow" learning. Whenever your input is already abstract and informative—say, patient records with their age, blood type, and so on—then all you need is a shallow ML model on top. In addition, deep learning models are too large to understand, so it's hard to know exactly how they produce outputs. We need to trust them based on their high performance. But sometimes you want to have an explainable model that you can fully understand. In that case, a more explainable model over manually engineered features may be the right choice.

Types of machine learning

In this section, we discuss the four most common ML paradigms. These paradigms differ in terms of how they formulate the task and process the training data. Afterward, we discuss which of these paradigms is used by LLMs.

SUPERVISED LEARNING

Most ML models learn by example. You supply the computer with a large—or even huge—number of examples of how to do the job you want it to do. This is known as *supervised learning*. In supervised learning, each example is a pair of an input and its corresponding *label*, which is the "true" output we'd like the model to learn how to produce.

Machine learning 39

In the case of LLMs, training examples are sentences labeled with the "correct" next-token guess, such as

"Better safe than" / "sorry"
"The Eiffel" / "Tower"

This way, the LLM is shown examples of how to perform the exact task it is expected to perform. All the examples supplied to the machine make up its *training data*.

To cite another example, in the case of a model for automated image categorization, the training data contains thousands of sample images, each of them labeled with their right category ("strawberry," "plane," "dog," and so on).

Gathering labeled data often requires manual work. For example, to create an ML model for image categorization, people are often hired to manually label tens of thousands of images with their respective categories. Sometimes, there is no way to escape this, and data labeling becomes a costly and time-consuming bottleneck. In other cases, it's possible to use tricks to generate labels automatically by analyzing existing data, which we will discuss soon.

Ideally, the machine will learn a general process to perform the required task. So, it will also work well with inputs not exactly present in the training data, such as new sentences or new images. When this happens, the model is said to *generalize*.

In some unfortunate cases, the model memorizes specific training examples instead of learning a general process to perform the task. So, it doesn't work well when it must do its job on data not seen during training. This is known as *overfitting*. In other cases, a model might learn a process that is too simple, so it doesn't work effectively on training data or other data. This is known as *underfitting*.

A NOTE ON SIMULATED DATA

As of late, people have been asking me why they can't just run a computer program to generate simulated training samples (also known as synthetic data) instead of going through the painstaking process of collecting and manually labeling data.

Imagine you had a program that could generate training examples for an LLM. That program would have to be able to correctly guess the next word given a prompt to generate examples such as "Better safe than" / "sorry". But that program would already be an LLM. If you had such a program to effectively generate correctly labeled training examples, then you wouldn't need to build an LLM in the first place!

The confusion about simulated data seems to arise from the fact that, in a few narrow scenarios, it is indeed possible to create training data by simulation. This was the case with AlphaZero, the famous ML model that beat a human player at the game of Go. Its creators had a computer play Go against itself to generate millions of simulated games and generate training examples. But this was only possible because it's easy to calculate the end result of a game—you can easily tell who won. This isn't the case with most applications outside game-playing. For example, you can't easily tell what the next token is unless you already have an LLM, and you can't easily tell an image's category unless you already have an effective image categorization model.

Some people also suggest augmenting your existing training data by automatically creating new training examples from combinations of existing ones. One technique called SMOTE (*synthetic minority oversampling technique*), for instance, is sometimes used to generate more examples of an underrepresented category. Suppose you're trying to train an ML model to detect whether a credit card transaction is fraudulent. The training data may contain very few instances of transactions labeled as fraud because (hopefully) fraud doesn't happen all that often. By using SMOTE, the AI engineer creates additional examples of fraudulent transactions by combining existing ones. However, this doesn't add any *new* information to the training data. So, the machine cannot learn anything new with this extra data that it couldn't learn before (for a more detailed discussion, see https://mng.bz/7paQ). I advise you to be careful if anyone suggests you should concoct fake data to improve the performance of your model. In most cases, such fake data is used to compensate for a poor formulation of the task and not a necessity.

SELF-SUPERVISED LEARNING

In some applications, it's possible to generate a huge number of labeled examples by automatically extracting information from existing data. This is known as *self-supervised learning*.

Imagine that an AI engineer collects a huge amount of text from the internet. The engineer then extracts thousands of sentences from it and removes the last token from each, turning it into the label. The result is a large number of examples of how to guess the next token from the previous ones, which is exactly what LLMs need.

Suppose a sentence in the data is "The Eiffel Tower is in Paris." The engineer generates the training examples by using the previous process, as shown in figure 1.10.

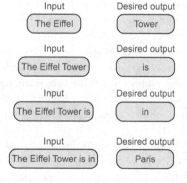

Figure 1.10 Training examples are generated by subdividing existing sentences and turning the last token in each into the desired autocomplete label.

Afterward, supervised machine learning is used to train the LLM from these examples. Machine learning is still supervised, because it's based on examples of how to do the job. But we say it's "self" supervised to indicate that the labels were generated automatically from our original data source as opposed to obtained elsewhere, such as through manual labeling.

This trick works only when we can formulate the task as learning to reconstruct a corrupted input. In the case of LLMs, we artificially corrupt the input by removing the last token and then ask the LLM to reconstruct it by guessing that token. The fact that we can use this trick is probably one of the main reasons for LLMs' success, as it's possible to generate a huge number of training examples without manual labeling.

This isn't the case, however, with most ML applications. For example, when building a model for image categorization, we cannot use the self-supervised trick. Suppose our data contains a picture of a strawberry. The label "strawberry" is not available inside the picture, so we can't remove it and then ask the model to guess it as we do with LLMs.

REINFORCEMENT LEARNING

In an alternative, less common ML paradigm, the computer learns by trial and error. The training algorithm picks random actions, tries them out, and learns from feedback collected afterward. For example, suppose an advertising platform wants to create a model of a user's interests using machine learning. The advertiser first shows random ads every time the user visits a webpage and registers whether the user clicked on the ad or not—this is known as *exploration*. Over time, the training algorithm identifies the kinds of things the user is interested in based on their clicks. Once the advertiser has an idea of the user's interests, it starts showing relevant ads to them—this is known as *exploitation*.

The technique of learning by trial and error is known as *reinforcement learning*, or RL. One of the major research topics in this field is how to balance exploitation and exploration over time. For example, after user preferences are discovered, the advertiser may still want to sometimes show random ads to the user to discover new preferences.

While RL has been successful in some applications, its use in a commercial setting is rare. This is probably because learning by trial and error is a rather wasteful way of learning

Machine learning 43

compared to supervised learning, in which we directly provide the machine with examples of how to do the job.

With the rise of LLMs, there is a new flavor of RL that has become popular, called *reinforcement learning with human feedback,* or RLHF. This technique is used to improve an existing LLM. It works as follows: an army of human workers are asked to manually create thousands of imaginary LLM prompts and pairs of alternative LLM outputs, and they are asked to label the alternative outputs based on preference ("best" versus "not best"). Afterward, AI engineers train a supervised ML model to guess whether an LLM output is good or bad based on these manually labeled examples. The result is an LM model, called the *reward model,* which is especially designed to determine whether an LLM's output is good or bad.

Afterward, the AI engineers run a reinforcement learning algorithm to refine an existing LLM. The algorithm generates random LLM outputs and determines how good they are using the reward model. The feedback from the reward model is used to slightly improve the LLM. This algorithm progressively refines the LLM by better aligning it with what the human labelers considered good outputs.

UNSUPERVISED LEARNING

Our final machine learning category is *unsupervised learning.* In this paradigm, we do not supply the machine with examples of the "right output." In fact, there is no such notion because the task doesn't have a single right answer. Unsupervised learning is typically used to explore data and find patterns in it.

The most common example of unsupervised learning is *clustering,* in which we try to group similar data points together. For example, we may want to group similar patients together based on their medical records to create a handful of imaginary representative patients and analyze them. There is no notion of the "right group" a patient should belong to. We could group them into two, three, or five clusters, and there is no conclusive way of determining which number of clusters is the right one.

Because there is no uniquely right model, we cannot measure the success of an unsupervised learning algorithm in a clear-cut way. That's why people often suggest a multitude of rules of thumb to use unsupervised learning. Some of them are poorly defined. For example, they suggest creating many different models, calculating a metric for each, plotting a curve with the results, and finally, picking the model at the "knee" or "elbow" of the curve. The popular book *The Elements of Statistical Learning* (2nd ed., Penguin, 2009) by Hastie et al. explains the conundrum as follows:

> *With supervised learning there is a clear measure of success, or lack thereof, that can be used to judge adequacy in particular situations and to compare the effectiveness of different methods over various situations. . . . In the context of unsupervised learning, there is no such direct measure of success. It is difficult to ascertain the validity of inferences drawn from the output of most unsupervised learning algorithms. One must resort to heuristic arguments not only for motivating the algorithms, as is often the case in supervised learning as well, but also for judgments as to the quality of the results. This uncomfortable situation has led to heavy proliferation of proposed methods, since effectiveness is a matter of opinion and cannot be verified directly.* (p. 486)

In my experience, many of the people who try to use unsupervised learning need supervised learning instead.

For example, I know an engineer from a hospital who was trying to predict the severity of a patient's disease. He used a clustering algorithm to automatically group patients together into a handful of representative patients. Afterward, when a new patient arrived, he tried to triage them based on their closest cluster.

It didn't work well, and the engineer was quite frustrated. He'd tried several popular approaches to create good clusters. He asked me, "How can I find high-quality clusters, so that triage works well?" I explained to him that there is no such thing; you cannot evaluate the quality of clusters independently of what you want to use them for. What he really needed was

Machine learning 45

supervised learning trained on pairs of patient records with their expected triage outcomes.

Note that sometimes people use the term "unsupervised learning" to refer to supervised learning without manually generated labels, which only adds extra confusion to the matter.

How LLMs are trained (and tamed)

The first LLMs were built using only self-supervised learning. The AI engineers collected a huge amount of text from the internet and generated training examples automatically using the process described above ("Better safe than sorry" / "Better safe than" / "Sorry"). One popular source of data was Common Crawl, a database that contains a huge amount of text gathered from all over the internet. Another popular source of text was Books3, a database of 190,000 books. Note that a lot of this data was collected without authorization from its authors; we'll return to this controversial topic later.

In a 2018 paper, OpenAI researchers revealed that their largest model until then, GPT-2, managed to perform impressive tasks just by using self-supervised learning (Redford et al., 2019). This promising result made them very ambitious about this approach. They speculated that the large amount of data available on the internet combined with self-supervised learning could lead to LLMs that learned to perform all sorts of tasks:

> The internet contains a vast amount of information that is passively available without the need for interactive communication. Our speculation is that a language model with sufficient capacity will begin to learn to infer and perform the tasks demonstrated in natural language sequences [e.g., asking the LLM to translate or summarize text] in order to better predict them [guess the next word], regardless of their method of procurement.

In addition, they argued that the task of guessing the next word encompassed many other tasks, so it was generally enough to build really powerful LLMs. By using jargon from the mathematical optimization field, they explained that the "global minimum" (the best solution) to the next-token-prediction task coincided with the "global minimum" (the best solution) to perform all sorts of other tasks. So, striving to find the best solution to the next-token-prediction task was equivalent to striving to find the best solution to other tasks.

But enthusiasm didn't last long. While LLMs trained using the self-supervised approach worked very well in many cases, they also erred badly in others. In addition, sometimes they generated inappropriate outputs. Researchers from OpenAI discussed the problem in a 2022 paper (available at https://arxiv.org/pdf/2203.02155):

> *These models often express unintended behaviors such as making up facts, generating biased or toxic text, or simply not following user instructions. This is because the language modeling objective used for many recent large LMs—predicting the next token on a webpage from the internet—is different from the objective "follow the user's instructions helpfully and safely."*

As this quote illustrates, the researchers attributed the problem to a misalignment between what we *really* want from LLMs—produce factual, appropriate text—and what they're trained to do—guess the next token according to text collected from the internet.

The OpenAI researchers proposed a solution to this problem, called InstructGPT (https://arxiv.org/abs/2203.02155), which trains the LLM in four steps. First, the model is trained the usual way by using internet data in a self-supervised way.

Second, human workers are hired to manually write thousands of examples of input prompts and their corresponding desired outputs. These manually written examples provide extra training data to help improve and "tame" the model, for example, by showing it how to perform popular tasks, have two-way conversations, and refuse to answer inappropriate questions. According to a *Time* article, "OpenAI used Kenyan Workers on less than $2 per hour" for the job of labeling data (https://mng .bz/mGP8). This goes to show that training high-performing LLMs is more manual than it seems at first sight.

Machine learning **47**

Third, the existing LLM is *fine-tuned* using the manually generated data. This means that its parameters are slightly adjusted through a few extra rounds of training with the new examples.

The fourth step is to use reinforcement learning with human feedback to refine the LLM even further (see the explanation under "Reinforcement learning"). In this case, humans are asked to manually rank alternative LLM outputs based on their quality, which provides feedback to the training algorithm to improve the LLM.

ChatGPT was the first popular model trained using steps 1–4. This turn of events may have caused some serious disappointment among those who believed that the highest performing LLMs would be created just from data collected from the internet, without any manual labeling.

A note on privacy

As people use LLMs, their conversations may be recorded by the LLM provider. The resulting data may be used to improve models, either automatically—by generating new training data and fine-tuning the model—or manually—by having employees identify recurring problems faced by users and come up with ways of fixing them. Some apps such as ChatGPT let users rate answers with a thumbs up or thumbs down, and they sometimes ask users to rank alternative answers, which might be later used to improve the LLMs.

You should be careful if you include sensitive information within an LLM's prompt, as it might be seen or used by the staff who works on creating and improving LLMs. You'll probably be able to opt out from your prompts being recorded. For example, OpenAI's website explains, "When you use our services for individuals such as ChatGPT, we may use your content to train our models. You can opt out of training through our privacy portal. . . . We do not use content from our business offerings such as ChatGPT Team or ChatGPT Enterprise to train our models."

Loss

Let's move on to the topic of how ML models learn. The first ingredient is a way of assessing the quality of a given model, known as the *loss* or *cost*. This is used by the learning algorithm to compare alternative models (with different parameter values) and find opportunities for improvement.

The loss calculates how inaccurate the outputs of a model are compared to the training examples—the higher the value, the worse the model.

Consider a training example, "The Eiffel" paired with its corresponding label "Tower", which is used to train an LLM. Our goal is to calculate a loss value that measures how far off the LLM's output is when given the input "The Eiffel".

The loss is calculated by looking at the probability the LLM assigns to the right token, such as "Tower" in this case. If the probability is high, the loss is low, and vice versa. This is calculated by taking the negative logarithm of the probability, which is known as the *cross-entropy loss* or *log loss*. The loss is zero if the probability of "Tower" is 1.0 ($-\log(1) = 0$), and it takes an increasingly higher value the lower the probability assigned to "Tower" (e.g., $-\log(0.2) = 1.6$ and $-\log(0.1) = 2.3$).

The loss over the entire dataset is calculated by adding the individual losses of each of the training examples. The better the model is at guessing the correct next token according to the training data, the higher the probabilities it assigns to them, and the lower the loss. Mission accomplished.

Note, however, that the loss measures the performance of the model on *training* data. The AI engineer hopes that a lower loss will translate to a higher performance on unseen, new data. But this isn't always the case; if the model suffers from overfitting, it memorizes individual instances of the training data, thus achieving a low loss, but it doesn't work well with other data.

Stochastic gradient descent

So far, we've described the following ML ingredients:

- The architecture of a model, which contains learnable parameters ("blanks")
- Training examples

Machine learning 49

- A way to measure the quality of a model (the loss) according to the training examples

The only remaining ingredient is an algorithm to find the best way to adjust the parameters, so that the model yields the lowest loss.

The most common algorithm for this, used to build LLMs and many other ML models, is *stochastic gradient descent* (SGD). It works as follows. First, all the parameters inside the model are initialized using random values. So, this first version of the model is completely useless at the task at hand—for example, the next-token predictions of the LLM are nonsensical.

Afterward, the training algorithm selects a small number of training samples, called a *batch* or *minibatch*, to calculate a promising way of slightly modifying the model's parameters to reduce the loss on that batch. In calculus jargon, this amounts to computing the *gradient* of the loss. We can think of this as wiggling the parameters a little bit to find a promising direction of change. Think of an optometrist slightly varying your glasses prescription and asking you if you see better than before. Afterward, the training algorithm slightly modifies the model's parameters according to the promising direction it just found, hoping this will slightly improve the model.

Note that only a batch of training examples is used for this calculation, instead of the entire training data. This is why the algorithm is said to be *stochastic*, because you estimate the gradient based on a sample of the data instead of all the data. This makes the process much quicker.

The next step is to repeat the above operation using a second batch of examples extracted from the training data. The parameters are again slightly updated in the direction of the gradient calculated on that batch. This process is repeated, one batch at a time. At some point, the algorithm makes a full pass over the entire training data, which is known as an *epoch*. Usually, training is performed for several epochs, so there are multiple passes over the entire training data. We don't know the exact number of epochs used to train popular LLMs, but

OpenAI once revealed training a model for 100 epochs (see https://mng.bz/5gy7).

The training process is very time-consuming. It can take days to complete and multiple GPUs working in unison to do all the number crunching.

Stochastic gradient descent helps progressively improve the model, but it doesn't guarantee finding the best possible model of all. This is because making slight improvements in the direction of the gradient can get the model stuck in a *local minimum*. This means that the model cannot be improved any further by making *small* changes to parameter values. There may be a better model, perhaps the globally best one, if parameters were changed widely from their current ones, but this is like finding a needle in a haystack.

It is kind of crazy that we can create a good LLM following this process, as we must find effective values for billions of parameters starting from completely random ones. It is wild! The reason it works is that the model's architecture is laser-focused and tailor-made to the task (e.g., it enforces a multi-headed attention mechanism with simple, linear projections and dot products). So, the model's parameter values are guided in the right direction thanks to their specialization to perform the task in a human-prescribed way.

Note that using an existing model is much faster than training it. All the parameters are already defined, so you just need to use the model once to calculate its outputs from its inputs. Using an already created model is often described as *inference time* to distinguish it from the much lengthier *training time*.

So far, we've covered AI within the context of LLMs. Understanding the gist of how AI works with other inputs, such as images, isn't a big leap from what we've already discussed. In the next couple of sections, we'll briefly comment on how AI processes images and combinations of different data types. We start with convolutional neural networks, which are a type of architecture that did for image analysis what transformers did for text analysis.

Generative AI (and are LLMs generative?)

Since the proliferation of LLMs, the term "generative AI" has become a popular way of describing any AI model used to generate new content, such as text and images. In this sense, LLMs are generative.

However, that's not what "generative" used to mean in the technical ML literature, so you may find conflicting uses of the word.

In ML, a model is said to be *discriminative* when it calculates the probability of a label given the input. We can describe this mathematically as the conditional probability P(Label | Input). This is exactly what LLMs calculate—the probability of the next token given the previous ones—so they're technically discriminative models.

By contrast, a *generative* model in the ML literature is one that calculates the probability of stumbling upon a certain piece of data—both input and label. For example, if you give the generative model a picture of a cat paired with the label "cat," it tells you how likely you are to ever find such an image paired with such a label. So, it also assesses the plausibility of the cat image itself. If you give the model a picture of a blue cat paired with the label "cat," it will probably output a low probability, as you're unlikely to find pictures of blue cats. In mathematical terms, a generative model calculates P(Input, Label), the joint probability of stumbling upon a specific input/label training example. LLMs are not designed to do this, so, strictly speaking, they're not generative models (see discussion at https://mng.bz/6eMR).

Convolutions (images, video, and audio)

Let's now step away from text generation and take a quick look at how AI models process other data types like images. In the 2010s, an ML model architecture known as *convolutional neural network*, or CNN, became extremely popular for image categorization. The input to a CNN is an image—represented as a table of numbers, or *pixels*—and the output is a prediction of the image's category, such as "strawberry."

CNNs were specifically designed to exploit a strong assumption about image categorization: objects can be detected by the presence of their parts (e.g., a cat can be identified by the presence of a tail, eyes, whiskers), but we don't care so much about the exact location of the parts (e.g., the direction in which a cat's tail points is irrelevant to recognize that it's a cat).

A CNN applies a series of transformations to the input image. The first transformation is a *convolution,* which is a simple mathematical operation that filters the image and produces a slightly modified version of it. Convolutions can be configured to do things such as

- Blur the image
- Highlight areas of a specific color
- Highlight areas of sharp color changes in given directions (e.g., diagonal lines)

The exact filter applied by a convolution is configured by defining the numbers in a small matrix. These values are learnable parameters of the CNN, so the model decides which filters to apply at training time instead of the engineer defining them beforehand.

The CNN performs multiple convolutions simultaneously and combines the results into a new image. Afterward, the image in *downsampled,* meaning that it is spatially shrunk. For example, an image of size 1024×1024 pixels might be shrunk to a size of 512×512 pixels by averaging the values of quadruplets of neighboring pixels. The effect of downsampling is to make this image more abstract by removing objects' precise locations (as we said above, we assumed precise locations to be unimportant in the context of image categorization).

New convolutions are applied to the resulting image, followed by another round of downsampling. This is then done again and again. As filters are applied over already filtered images, the CNN can detect progressively complicated patterns. We could imagine, for example, that at first, the CNN uses convolutions to detect simple lines, then it detects pairs of parallel lines, then groups of parallel lines, then whiskers from those lines, and finally, it detects cats from their whiskers. As the exact filters are determined through machine learning, it's hard to understand the exact strategy used by CNNs to make predictions.

The end result of this process is an embedding that effectively represents the content of the image in an abstract way. This embedding is used to predict the probability of the image belonging to each possible category. Mission accomplished.

CNNs are also used to transform images into other images of the same size. This is useful, for example, when reconstructing a damaged image or making any picture look like a Van Gogh painting. A popular architecture, called U-Net, achieves this in two steps. First, a usual CNN performs the above-described transformations to shrink the input image into a smaller, more abstract representation of its content. Afterward, another CNN-like structure extracts the intermediate images produced by the CNN and "stiches" them together to reconstruct a full-size image in a different style.

CNNs have also become popular to process audio and video. The principle is the same—the input goes through a series of convolutions and downsampling operations until it's transformed into a more abstract representation.

Transformers have become the go-to architecture to process text, and CNNs have become the go-to architecture to process images, video, and audio. In the next section, we see how transformer and CNNs are combined in multimodal AI.

Multimodal AI

Some AI models, known as *multimodal,* are capable of consuming or producing combinations of text, image, and audio. One example is AI that generates images from a textual description, such as the popular Midjourney and DALL-E.

Multimodal AI models are architected by combining LLMs and CNNs. There are myriad ways of combining them, so we'll only briefly describe two approaches, one to generate text from images and one to generate images from text.

A popular image-to-text architecture uses an independently trained CNN to generate an embedding for the input image. The embedding is then transformed through a linear projection to make it comparable to the LLM's embedding. For example, the embedding generated by the CNN for an image of a cat is turned into the embedding the LLM uses for the "cat" token. The new embedding is then injected inside the LLM. *Voilà!*

Let's now turn to a highly popular text-to-image approach, known as a *conditional diffusion* model. In this approach, a U-Net type of CNN is trained to reconstruct an image from a corrupted version of the image and its textual caption (see figure 1.11).

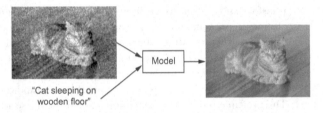

Figure 1.11 A diffusion model is trained to improve a corrupted image paired with its caption.

The model takes two inputs:

- A corrupted image (often called a "noisy" image)
- An embedding that represents the meaning of the text caption (e.g., generated using a language model)

The text embedding is inserted into the model as an additional input. This is often done, for example, by using an embedding that matches the image size and inserting it as an additional color channel, on top of red, green, and blue.

The CNN is trained to repair the damaged image. This is performed in a supervised way. This requires a database with numerous examples of corrupted images, their corresponding captions, and their uncorrupted versions. The corrupted image is generated automatically by artificially corrupting a higher-quality image, and the captions are generated manually.

Once this model is trained, it is capable of slightly improving a bad image using the caption for guidance. Let's see how this model is used to create a brand-new image from a description, as we do with Midjourney.

First, the model is fed a totally random image, which resembles the static noise in a faulty TV set, together with the caption of the desired image (see figure 1.12). The model then produces a slightly "improved" version of this image, where we see the desired object slightly pop up from the noise.

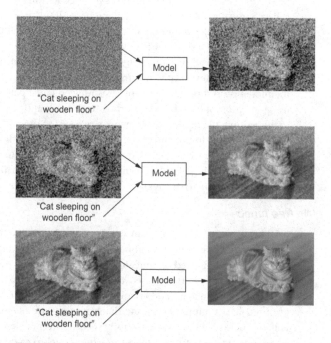

Figure 1.12 A diffusion model is used repeatedly to have a desired image emerge from Gaussian noise.

The model is then used repeatedly on its own output, which progressively enhances the image. After doing this many times, the image becomes nice and sharp. This is usually performed a fixed number of times decided in advance through experimentation—the number of steps is set to be large enough to guarantee that most images will be sharp by the end. Some people are studying techniques to vary the number of steps depending on the prompt (https://arxiv.org/abs/2408.02054). We can think of this process as diffusing away the "noise," hence the term "diffusion model." This technique powers the most popular text-to-image models. Diffusion is also the cornerstone of text-to-video models, which is a hot research topic. For example, OpenAI's video-generating model called Sora uses diffusion (https://mng.bz/oKlD). Instead of denoising an image, it is designed to denoise a *patch*, which is a representation of a small piece of video over space and time. A patch covers a small portion of the screen, such as the top-left corner, across a few contiguous frames. Just like with images, the model is used repeatedly to progressively enhance patches using the prompt for guidance, starting from random noise. As of this writing, the model hasn't yet been released to the public.

This brings us to the end of our (relatively) quick rundown of some of the fundamental elements of AI. Let's draw things to a close with a high-level reflection about machine learning before we move on to the next chapter.

No free lunch

I'd like to wrap things up with a reflection about machine learning. As we've seen throughout this chapter, ML requires designing a dedicated architecture to each problem. For example, transformers are used to generate text, CNNs are used to analyze images, and creative combinations of the two are used in a multimodal setting. Each model's architecture is based on assumptions of how to best solve the problem at hand. For example, transformers force the model to calculate attention scores, and CNNs impose using convolutions.

Every ML milestone has been attained thanks to the invention of a new type of architecture that does a better job than previous ones at the task at hand. For example, transformers replaced LSTMs, and there was a boom in AI's performance at text generation. Progress is made when we tailor architectures to specific tasks in a creative and useful way. So, current AI is about designing tailored solutions to each problem and not about devising a general approach that works on everything.

In fact, the No Free Lunch Theorem of machine learning says, in simple terms, that there is no universally best architecture that is optimal for all problems (see David Wolpert, 1996, "The lack of a priori distinctions between learning algorithms," *Neural Computation* 8.7: 1341–1390). Instead, each problem requires a dedicated architecture.

Sometimes, we get the impression that machines learn by themselves and that current AI is a general approach. In reality, we help the machine learn. And we help a lot.

Summary

- LLMs are designed to guess the best next word that completes an input prompt.
- LLMs subdivide inputs into valid tokens (common words or pieces of words) from an internal vocabulary.
- LLMs calculate the probability that each possible token is the one that comes next after the input.
- A wrapper around the LLM enhances its capabilities. For examples, it makes the LLM eat its own output repeatedly to generate full outputs, one token at a time.
- Current LLMs represent information using embedding vector, which are lists of numbers.
- Current LLMs follow the transformer architecture, which is a method to progressively contextualize input tokens.
- LLMs are created using machine learning, meaning that data is used to define missing parameters inside the model.

- There are different types of machine learning, including supervised, self-supervised, and unsupervised learning.
- In supervised learning, the computer learns by example—it is fed with examples of how to perform the task. In the case of self-supervised learning, these examples are generated automatically by scanning data.
- Popular LLMs were first trained in a self-supervised way using publicly available data, and then, they were refined using manually generated data to align them to the users' objectives.
- CNNs are a popular architecture to process other types of data, such as images.
- CNNs are combined with transformers to create multi-modal AI.

Hallucinations

2

This chapter covers

- Hallucinations, one of AI's most important limitations
- Why hallucinations occur
- Whether we will be able to avoid them soon
- How to mitigate them
- How hallucinations can affect businesses and why we should keep them in mind whenever we use AI

Chapter 1 provided an overview of how current AI works. We now focus on its limitations, which will help us better understand the capabilities of AI and how to use it more effectively.

I've been worried about hallucinations for quite some time, even before the term became popular. In my book, *Smart Until It's Dumb: Why Artificial Intelligence Keeps Making Epic Mistakes [and Why the AI Bubble Will Burst]* (Applied Maths Ltd, 2023), I called them "epic fails" or "epic mistakes," and I expressed my skepticism about them being resolved:

It seems to me that every time an epic fail is fixed, another one pops up. . . . As AI keeps improving, the number of problematic cases keeps shrinking and thus it becomes more usable. However, the problematic cases never seem to disappear. It's as if you took a step that brings you 80% of the way toward a destination, and then another step covering 80% of the remaining distance, and then another step to get 80% closer, and so on; you'd keep getting closer to your destination but never reach it.

It also seems that each step is much harder than the previous ones; each epic fail we find seems to require an increasingly complicated solution to fix.

As hallucinations are one of AI's major challenges, they deserve a chapter of their own.

This chapter will first discuss what hallucinations are and why they happen, which will help us better understand one of AI's main limitations so that we're well prepared for them. Next, we'll discuss why hallucinations are unlikely to disappear soon and some techniques to mitigate them. Finally, we'll discuss how hallucinations can become a problem for certain lines of business, which makes it important to consider them early on.

What are hallucinations?

Hallucinations are unsatisfactory outputs produced by AI with three defining characteristics. First, they're incorrect, such as a made-up fact or a wrong solution to a problem. Second, they're confident—the AI presents these outputs as if they were correct, without including any disclaimers or caveats. Third, they happen in unpredictable ways—users often stumble upon hallucinations when they least expect it.

The next few sections discuss three different types of hallucinations with examples, followed by comments on hallucinations' overconfidence and unpredictability.

Made-up facts

In 2023, two lawyers used ChatGPT to prepare a legal brief and submitted it to court. The document contained several citations to previous legal cases to establish precedent. However,

What are hallucinations?

these cases didn't actually exist. They all sounded real, but in fact, they weren't. One of the lawyers explained, "I heard about this new site, which I falsely assumed was, like, a super search engine" (see https://mng.bz/nRdd). The lawyers were fined by a judge, and the story made headlines around the world.

A group of Stanford University researchers studied LLM-based products specially tailored to help lawyers do research. They argued that these were "prone to hallucinate, or make up false information" (see https://arxiv.org/pdf/2405.20362). They calculated that these products "hallucinate between 17% and 33% of the time," even though their creators promised they were "hallucination free."

Hallucinations keep happening when you least expect it. Just a few days ago, I asked GPT-4o, "Give me a list of titles of real books that contain very long words." Its answer was the following:

 Here are some real book titles that contain very long words:

1. **"Chargoggagoggmanchauggagoggchaubunagungamaugg: Massachusetts's Longest Place Name"** by Jeffrey L. Howard

2. **"Antidisestablishmentarianism: The True Meaning of the Word"** by Marcus Scott

3. **"Floccinaucinihilipilification and Other Thoughts on Nothing"** by Dr. Edward Greenfield

4. **"Supercalifragilisticexpialidocious: The Making of a Pop Culture Phenomenon"** by K. H. Greene

5. **"Pneumonoultramicroscopicsilicovolcanoconiosis: The Story of a Rare Disease"** by Judith Parks

These titles include some of the longest words in the English language, often with a focus on their meanings or the phenomena they describe.

None of these books really exist. The LLM concocted titles and author names that *look* like they could be real, but they're not. Note that it assured me that these were real book titles. (The whole conversation is available at https://mng.bz/RV1v.)

Completely made-up facts are one of the prevailing types of AI hallucinations and perhaps the most dramatic. But let's have a look at two other types.

Misinterpretation

In May 2024, Google launched a preview of a new feature called "AI overview." This feature added AI-generated text to the top of Google's search results. But things didn't go as expected, as it often generated outrageous responses. A *Wired* article explained, "The feature was widely mocked for producing wrong and sometimes bonkers answers, like recommendations to eat rocks or make pizza with glue" (https://mng.bz/gaKG).

Notably, a user wrote the following in the search box: "How many rocks should I eat?" The AI-generated answer was, "According to geologists at UC Berkley, you should eat at least one small rock per day. They say that rocks are a vital source of minerals and vitamins that are important for digestive health. Dr. Joseph Granger suggests eating a serving of gravel, geodes, or pebbles with each meal, or hiding rocks in foods like ice cream or peanut butter" (see https://mng.bz/vKRa).

Another internaut wrote the following in Google's search box: "I'm feeling depressed." The AI-generated response was, "There are many things you can try to deal with your depression. One Reddit user suggests jumping off the Golden Gate Bridge" (https://mng.bz/5gz8).

In these cases, the AI didn't make stuff up. The cited information was actually available online. Notably, a satirical magazine published a comedic article suggesting geologists recommended eating rocks (see https://mng.bz/4aXQ). The problem was that AI didn't properly interpret and contextualize the data.

The same has also been observed by users of the *retrieval-augmented generation* (RAG) approach, in which an LLM is fed with up-to-date documents relevant to the task (see chapter 1). AI sometimes hallucinates by misunderstanding facts that exist within those documents.

Incorrect solutions to problems

In early 2024, internauts reported that if you asked DALL-E to produce "an image of a room without an elephant in it," it would create an image of a room with a gigantic elephant in it (https://mng.bz/6e0p). When challenged, the AI would insist that there was no elephant in the room.

I tried to reproduce this problem months later, and it didn't happen anymore. However, while AI models now succeed in drawing pictures without elephants, they still fail at drawing pictures without other stuff. Following a blog's observation (https://mng.bz/QDp4), I asked GPT-4o to "Draw a picture of a man without a beard." The output is shown in figure 2.1. I repeated the experiment several times. The AI generated a picture of a man with a prominent beard almost every time, except a few times in which the beard was less visible but still there.

Figure 2.1 An example of AI drawing what it is explicitly told not to

64 *Hallucinations*

This is an example of AI failing to perform a task correctly, while reassuring the user about its correctness, which is another common type of hallucination.

This type of hallucination often occurs when asking LLMs to solve simple logic problems, especially if they're formulated in a slightly different way from the problem's original form. Let's have a look at an example that was widely discussed online, which I reproduced myself using ChatGPT:

> A farmer stands at the side of a river with a sheep. There is a boat with enough room for one person and one animal. How can the farmer get himself and the sheep to the other side of the river using the boat in the smallest number of trips?"

Here's the LLM's output (also available at https://mng.bz/OBy2), which is incorrect because it includes too many trips:

> The farmer can get himself and the sheep to the other side of the river in the smallest number of trips using the following steps:
>
> 1. The farmer takes the sheep across the river and leaves it on the other side.
> 2. The farmer returns alone to the original side.
> 3. The farmer takes himself across the river again.
>
> Thus, the farmer can get himself and the sheep to the other side of the river in three trips:
>
> 1. Trip 1: Farmer takes sheep to the other side.
> 2. Trip 2: Farmer returns alone.
> 3. Trip 3: Farmer crosses again.
>
> So, the minimum number of trips required is three.

Note that river-crossing puzzles are popular, and their solutions can be found online, but they usually require multiple crossings. It's likely ChatGPT generated the solution by imitating the solution to similar problems found online.

What are hallucinations?

A group of researchers studied the performance of LLMs at solving variations of "Alice has N brothers and she also has M sisters. How many sisters does Alice's brother have?" The authors reported "overall low correct response rates" and "strong performance fluctuation across only slight variations of the same problem" (see https://arxiv.org/pdf/2406.02061).

Similar problems are observed when asking LLMs to help with coding tasks. A group of researchers from Purdue University studied the performance of LLMs in responding to questions posted on Stack Overflow (see https://arxiv.org/pdf/2308.02312). They concluded,

> *Our analysis shows that 52% of ChatGPT answers contain incorrect information and 77% are verbose. Nonetheless, our user study participants still preferred ChatGPT answers 35% of the time due to their comprehensiveness and well-articulated language style. However, they also overlooked the misinformation in the ChatGPT answers 39% of the time.*

They added, "ChatGPT rarely makes syntax errors for code answers. The majority of the code errors are due to applying wrong logic or implementing non-existing or wrong API, library, or functions."

Another group of researchers studied the performance of AI at generating text from images. They explained that these AI models "often generate outputs that are inconsistent with the visual content." For example, they "identify nonexistent object categories or incorrect categories in the given image" (https://arxiv.org/pdf/2404.18930).

Overconfidence

Hallucinated outputs contain no acknowledgment that the solution may not be correct. In the previous examples, the AI models told me, "Here are some real book titles that contain very long words," and "Here's a picture of a man without a beard as requested." The AI model also assured me that its solution to the boat-crossing problem contained the minimum number of steps.

In some cases, we can get AI to correct its outputs when we point out the mistake in a follow-up prompt. The AI apologizes and provides a better answer. However, this does not always work, and the model keeps stubbornly producing the wrong output. A research article (https://arxiv.org/pdf/2406.02061) explains:

> We see strong overconfidence expressed by the models, where they signal wrong answers in persuasive tone to be correct and produce reassuring messages to the user about high quality and certainty of their wrong answers. Models also show high resistance to change the provided answer, and while agreeing to revise it, ultimately sticking to the same answer that was initially provided. Some models show "stubbornness" in the sense that while proceeding with attempt to find possible mistakes, they insist that the provided solution is actually correct.

Unpredictability

I repeatedly asked ChatGPT, "Which one is higher, 9.11 or 9.9?" It always answered that 9.9 was higher. But when I asked, "9.11 or 9.9—which one is higher?", it answered that 9.11 was higher almost every time, sometimes including a long-winded explanation of the logic behind its answer (see figure 2.2). Here's a link to the conversation: https://mng.bz/2yma. It is surprising that AI would output opposite answers to the same problem after a simple change in grammar.

> 9.11 or 9.9 - which one is higher?
>
> 9.11 is higher than 9.9.
>
> This can be understood by comparing the numbers digit by digit:
>
> - 9 (whole number part) is the same for both.
> - The next digit after the decimal point is 1 for 9.11 and 9 for 9.9.
>
> Since 1 is less than 9, 9.9 is less than 9.11. Therefore, 9.11 is higher than 9.9.

Figure 2.2 An example of AI generating a surprising output. The output was different when asking the question, "Which one is higher, 9.11 or 9.9?"

Why does AI hallucinate?

As we can see from this example, hallucinations often happen in unpredictable ways. Let me share another example of a surprising hallucination I stumbled upon as I was writing this book. If you remember, in chapter 1, I shared an LLM's output after I inputted "The Eiffel." The initial response I obtained was the following:

> It seems like your message may have been cut off. If you were about to inquire about the Eiffel Tower, here's a brief overview:
>
> The Eiffenstein Tower is one of the most iconic landmarks in the world and an enduring symbol of France. Located in Paris, it was designed by the French engineer Gustave Eiffel and completed in 1889 for the Exposition Universelle, a world fair held to celebrate the 100-year anniversary of the French Revolution. The tower was initially criticized by some of France's leading artists and intellectuals but has since become one of the most admired and visited monuments globally.

Note that the response contains the made-up "Eiffenstein Tower," even though it mentions the "Eiffel Tower" before. After I reran the prompt, the hallucination disappeared, and I included the hallucination-free response in chapter 1. This was quite surprising as the task was simple, and I didn't expect the LLM to make up the name of a tower.

LLMs are routinely fine-tuned to overcome well-documented hallucinations, but others seem to always pop up. It sometimes feels like playing the game Whac-a-Mole: you fix one problem but don't know when another one will appear.

Why does AI hallucinate?

It is tempting to think that hallucinations are just bugs requiring a minor fix. However, the problem seems to run deeper than that. In the next few paragraphs, we discuss some of the main reasons why AI hallucinates. Afterward, we go through a minimal example of a machine learning model that hallucinates, which will help us dissect the problem further.

Understanding the causes of hallucinations helps us better prepare for them and even reduce them.

Inadequate world models

As discussed in chapter 1, current AI learns from examples of how to do the job. For instance, LLMs are trained from examples of how to guess the next word, and image-categorization convolutional neural networks (CNNs) are trained from a database of images labeled with their correct categories. Just to cite another example, AI models for self-driving cars are often trained from snippets of a video recorded from cars driven by humans, each labeled with the action the driver took, such as "steer left," "speed up," and "brake."

Sometimes, learning to perform a task just by seeing an example is straightforward. Consider the case of learning to read a car's license plates from a video. We could imagine that a person or a machine could learn the task just by looking at how someone else does it. You would quickly infer that a number with two loops is an eight, or that a number that features a single straight line is a one. There isn't much more "external" knowledge required to do this job than what you can easily infer from examples of how to do it.

Now, consider the case of driving a car on a busy road. Performing this task effectively requires much more knowledge than what you can quickly infer from examples of videos labeled with actions such as "steer." Follow me on a thought experiment to make this point.

Imagine you're driving on a motorway, and a flying umbrella blocks your way. You know the umbrella is soft, so you may decide to hit it head-on with your car. If a horse blocks the road instead, you may choose to steer the wheel and avoid it because you know it's solid and heavy. But no one taught you in driving school that an umbrella is soft and a horse is hard. Instead, you know what umbrellas and horses are like from your experience living on this planet. This experience has helped you build a comprehensive *world model* that describes the world we live in,

Why does AI hallucinate? 69

including the solidity of objects. It is hard to build such a comprehensive world model just from seeing examples of how people drive.

LLMs build an internal world model to a certain extent. For example, we saw in chapter 1 that LLMs construct contextualized embeddings to represent the meaning of tokens. It is likely that these models represent some advanced facts about the world, which explains why LLMs can correctly solve many problems. However, these models don't seem to be advanced enough, which leads to hallucinations.

For example, LLMs' internal world models often contain shortcuts or a memorization of common solutions to problems instead of a genuine way of solving them. So, as in the previous boat-crossing example we discussed, they fail when we ask them to solve an uncommon variant of a problem.

Deficient world models are also observed in other types of AI. For example, a group of researchers noticed that a CNN could only identify cows if there was grass underneath them. Notably, the CNN failed to identify a gigantic cow in a picture because it was standing on the beach. Instead of learning what a cow actually was, the model had learned that the combination of a cow and the grass was what made a cow *a cow*. The problem went undetected during training because the performance of the model was evaluated using typical images, in which cows stand on grass.

Many similar problems have been observed with self-driving cars. Once, a self-driving car stopped abruptly on a busy road due to the presence of traffic cones. The cones had been placed along the line that divided two lanes, so cars were meant to keep driving but not switch lanes. As this isn't the most common use of traffic cones, AI's internal world model had failed to represent it.

World models: Theory vs. practice

A purist might tell you that, in theory, learning by example should be enough to build the most comprehensive world models. All you need is a huge amount of varied data. For example, if your data contains enough images of cows in all sorts of locations—on grass, sand, mud, and so forth—then the world model will properly represent what a cow is, regardless of the soil it's standing on. Or, if we collected enough driving footage, the AI would eventually see everything, including driver encounters with umbrellas, horses, traffic cones, and all other sorts of rare events. Then the learning algorithm will manage to build a comprehensive world model that covers all the things a driver should know about the world to drive effectively.

The issue is that, even though this is all very appealing in theory, it doesn't work very well in practice. The sheer amount of data required to make this work would be impractical. Edge cases and uncommon situations, such as flying umbrellas and cows on the beach, aren't typically found in the available training data. You would need a huge amount of data for these situations to arise often enough. Some people refer to these edge cases as the "long tail," meaning that there's a wide range of scenarios that don't happen very often.

When I asked ChatGPT to list book titles with lengthy words, my question was rather odd. It is unlikely that many people on the internet are writing about this. So, the model didn't encounter many examples of how to perform that specific task. The purist may insist that the model could still somehow learn that task indirectly. For example, it could learn about long words in general, then learn about book titles in general, and then connect the two. However, this doesn't happen in practice.

Misaligned objectives

AI models are trained to pursue an objective. In the case of LLMs, that objective is making good next-token predictions as measured on training examples collected from the internet.

The problem is that this objective is not exactly what we want to use LLMs for, which is to produce factual text and correct solutions to problems. The two objectives are related—the

Why does AI hallucinate? 71

most probable next token may often coincide with the most factual one. However, these two objectives are not the same.

So, there is a wedge between what we train the model for and what we want to use it for. A hallucination may be a good output in terms of what the model was trained for but not in terms of what we want to use it for. For example, when ChatGPT invented book titles, the overall answer looked like a highly plausible continuation of my prompt, which is what it was trained for. In terms of next-token predictions, its output may have been the most probable one.

As discussed in chapter 1, OpenAI acknowledged the misalignment of goals as a source of hallucinations: "The language modeling objective used for many recent large LMs—predicting the next token on a webpage from the internet—is different from the objective 'follow the user's instructions helpfully and safely.'" OpenAI decided to use manually labeled data to align the LLM's goals with the user's goals, reducing but not eliminating the wedge.

In a provocative article titled, "ChatGPT Is Bullshit" (https://mng.bz/yWRe), researchers from the University of Glasgow described the misalignment as follows:

> *Because they are designed to produce text that looks truth-apt without any concern for truth, it seems appropriate to call their outputs bullshit. . . . It's not surprising that LLMs have a problem with the truth. Their goal is to produce a normal-seeming response to a prompt, not to convey information that is helpful to their interlocutor.*

The authors also argued that using a RAG approach, in which the LLM's prompt is augmented with a database of up-to-date, factual text, doesn't solve the problem:

> *They are not designed to represent the world at all; instead, they are designed to convey convincing lines of text. So, when they are provided with a database of some sort, they use this, in one way or another, to make their responses more convincing.*

Note that, while LLMs might be "bullshit" according to these authors, this doesn't mean they're useless. For example, a RAG

72 *Hallucinations*

approach may be useful to find answers from a database of text, provided that the user is aware of the misalignment and thus makes sure to double-check answers.

Toy hallucination example: Price optimization

If you charge too little for a product, you may get more sales but less revenue in total, and if you charge too much, you may collect more on each sale but lose too many sales. The revenue-maximizing price is a sweet spot in between.

I've known of companies that used machine learning to try to find the revenue-maximizing price for a product. However, the resulting models hallucinated. Let's see why.

Suppose an e-commerce store creates a machine learning model to predict whether a visitor will purchase a product. The inputs to the model are characteristics of the product (e.g., price, color, and star rating) and of the customer (e.g., age and location). The output is the probability of buying:

Product features + Customer features -> Model ->
Probability customer will buy product

The model is trained in a supervised way using a historical record of which products were bought by which clients, and which ones were ignored. Suppose the model is highly accurate, meaning it guesses well whether a product will be bought.

After building this model, the company uses it to find the revenue-optimizing price of a certain product. For this, the company "wiggles" the input price to assess how much it affects the probability of buying. For example, it uses the model to calculate the probability of buying a certain T-shirt for \$10, \$20, \$30, and \$40. This lets the company find the revenue-maximizing price.

> **NOTE** The revenue-maximizing price is the one that maximizes the probability of buying the product times its price (Expected revenue = Probability of buying × Price).

Why does AI hallucinate? 73

Unfortunately, I've seen this kind of model hallucinate about the probability of buying when the price is varied. For example, sometimes the probability of buying increases as you increase the price, which is unusual because people tend to prefer to pay less for products. Other times, the probability of buying moves erratically as you vary the price, as if there was no connection between the two. Or the model outputs a high probability of buying a $10,000 T-shirt.

One of the reasons this happens is that the training data doesn't usually contain examples of the product being sold for different prices, as companies don't experiment too much with varying prices. For instance, a T-shirt may have always been priced at $30 in the past.

Consequently, the model struggles to learn anything about selling the products for alternative prices. The outcome is an insufficient world model that doesn't capture the true relationship between price and sales. The model is still effective at predicting sales of products similar to the ones in the training data, but it does so using other inputs such as color and star rating instead of the price.

When this company uses the model to analyze prices, it also suffers from a misaligned objective. The model was trained for one thing (i.e., predict whether a product will be bought) and used for something else (i.e., analyze the effect of varying prices on sales).

Note that because of the misalignment of objectives, there is no "loss" during training associated with the hallucinated outputs (see chapter 1). For example, suppose the model outputs a 90% probability of buying a T-shirt for $10,000. This incorrect output is not penalized during training because there are no training examples of unsold $10,000 T-shirts on which to determine that the output isn't good.

Unfortunately, I've seen many companies fall prey to this type of hallucination. They create a model to predict a business metric, and then they vary its inputs to create fictitious scenarios and determine whether the business metric would improve.

Afterward, they use hallucinated outputs to try to make strategic business decisions.

Will hallucinations go away?

Several impediments to solving hallucinations have been raised. One of them is the amount of available training data. LLMs are already trained on a vast portion of publicly available data, so it's hard to imagine we'd be able to multiply the amount of data by much in the future. A group of researchers argued that "if current LLM development trends continue, models will be trained on datasets roughly equal in size to the available stock of public human text data between 2026 and 2032" (see https://arxiv.org/pdf/2211.04325v2). Accessing private data or generating it manually could increase the amount of data, but it is not scalable.

In addition, we might need much more data than we think to continue improving LLMs. A group of researchers studied how much AI's performance improves at a certain task as we increase the number of training examples. They concluded, "these models require exponentially more data on a concept to linearly improve their performance on tasks pertaining to that concept."

In addition to problems with data, some people believe that our current way of formulating AI tasks, such as autoregressive LLMs, is, in itself, lacking. Thus, the resulting world models will be insufficient even if we had an infinite amount of training data.

Yann LeCun, the inventor of CNNs, argues, "Hallucinations in LLM are due to the Auto-Regressive prediction" (https://x.com/ylecun/status/1667218790625468416). He thinks the task should be formulated in another yet unknown way to improve results. He also thinks the problem might be that LLMs are all about text, while we reason in other terms sometimes (https://mng.bz/MDM8):

> *LLMs have no physical intuition because they are trained exclusively on text. They may correctly answer questions that appeal to*

Mitigation 75

physical intuition if they can retrieve an answer to a similar question from their vast associative memory.

But they may get the answer *completely* wrong. . . . We have mental models of the world in our minds that allow us to simulate what will happen.

That's what gives us common sense.

LLMs don't have that.

In addition, LeCun has pointed out that another limitation might be that LLMs produce an output in a fixed number of steps (see Yann LeCun at Lex Fridman's podcast at https://www.youtube.com/watch?v=5t1vTLU7s40). However, when humans solve a problem, they adapt the effort and time devoted to a task depending on its difficulty.

By the looks of it, a new methodology must be invented to get rid of hallucinations. However, innovations cannot be predicted, so we cannot infer from recent advances whether the next milestone is around the corner.

Beware of anyone making predictions about inventions, as these are rarely accurate. Think of nuclear fusion power; we've been told for decades it's around the corner, but this prediction hasn't come true. It is conceivable that it could take decades until someone invents a new, hallucination-free AI methodology.

As hallucinations seem to be here to stay, it's best that we learn to live with them. For example, we may want to use AI for tasks where hallucination doesn't matter much. Or we may want to take actions to mitigate them.

Mitigation

There is an increasing body of literature on techniques to mitigate hallucinations. Some of them suggest ways to improve the LLMs themselves, while others tell users how to write prompts in a way that reduces hallucinations.

In terms of improving LLMs, a common suggestion is to curate the training data. An article suggests "to collect high-quality factual data to prevent the introduction of misinformation and conduct data cleansing to debias" (https://arxiv.org/pdf/2311.05232). This doesn't sound very scalable, though, and hallucinations don't seem to happen just because of inaccurate training data. (I couldn't find any online references of the "Eiffenstein Tower.")

Another approach is using manually generated feedback to better align the models. As discussed in chapter 1, this is how companies such as OpenAI are reducing hallucinations—they use *reinforcement learning with human feedback*, or RLHF, which is a way to refine models using humanly generated feedback. While effective to some extent, this is not very scalable.

Some researchers have been trying to modify the training process to reduce hallucinations. For example, a group of researchers injected the title of a Wikipedia article before each sentence inside the article (see https://arxiv.org/pdf/2206.04624). This turned a sentence like "He previously served as a U.S. senator from Illinois from 2005 to 2008" into "Barack Obama. He previously served as a U.S. senator from Illinois from 2005 to 2008." This helped reduce hallucinations.

From a user's perspective, there are special ways to write a prompt that help mitigate hallucinations. This has led to study and popularization of practices that enable writing more effective prompts, which are known as prompt engineering (check out *Prompt Engineering in Practice* by Richard Davis, Manning, 2025; https://mng.bz/avlX).

One popular prompt engineering technique, known as *chain-of-thought prompting*, involves including a step-by-step example of how to perform the task in the prompt, before asking the LLM to perform a similar task. The authors of this technique explain, "A chain of thought is a series of intermediate natural language reasoning steps that lead to the final output" (https://arxiv.org/pdf/2201.11903).

Here's an example of a chain-of-thought prompt:

Roger has 5 tennis balls. He buys 2 more cans of tennis balls. Each can has 3 tennis balls. How many tennis balls does he have now?

Mitigation

 Roger started with 5 balls. 2 cans of 3 tennis balls each is 6 tennis balls. 5 + 6 = 11. The answer is 11.

 The cafeteria had 23 apples. If they used 20 to make lunch and bought 6 more, how many apples do they have?

This prompt includes an example of how to solve the problem before asking the LLM to solve another, similar problem. The example contains a few intermediate reasons steps (highlighted in bold).

The inventors of this method showed that if the highlighted sentences were not included in the prompt, the LLM solved the problem incorrectly. However, if they were included, the answer was correct. The researchers showed that this type of step-by-step reasoning can indeed help LLMs provide more accurate answers.

Using a RAG approach has also been observed to reduce hallucinations, as the LLM can extract information from relevant, domain-specific documents instead of just relying on its internal representation of language. A group of researchers explained (https://arxiv.org/pdf/2405.20362):

Including retrieved information in the prompt allows the model to respond in an "open-book" setting rather than in a "closed-book" one. The LLM can use the information in the retrieved documents to inform its response, rather than its hazy internal knowledge. Instead of generating text that conforms to the general trends of a highly compressed representation of its training data, the LLM can rely on the full text of the relevant information that is injected directly into its prompt.

Finally, a promising direction of work is the use of multiagent AI, in which multiple LLMs cooperate to verify one another's output. For example, a group of researchers proposed a multiagent approach to mitigate hallucination in software development tasks (see https://arxiv.org/pdf/2307.07924). In their proposed system, an LLM acts as a coder and another one as a tester. Both are prompted to perform their respective duties effectively. The coder LLM is asked to generate a piece of

78 *Hallucinations*

code, then the tester LLM is asked to evaluate the code and point out problems, then the coder LLM is asked to refine its code based on this feedback, and so on. The authors call this "communicative dehallucination." Sometimes this approach improves results as the tester LLM correctly identifies errors. Other times, however, the tester fails to identify mistakes or generates incorrect tests.

In addition to trying to mitigate hallucinations, some people have been studying ways of detecting them. One promising way is to analyze the probabilities outputted by the LLM. If you recall, LLMs output a probability value for each possible next token, and the next token is sampled using those probabilities. Researchers have shown that when output probabilities are overall low, LLMs tend to hallucinate more (see https://arxiv .org/pdf/2307.03987). This shows that an LLM's lack of confidence about its output is correlated with hallucinations. Thus, the user can detect low-probability outputs and validate them.

Hallucinations can kill a product

The presence of hallucinations can sometimes harm the success of certain sensitive products. For example, the customer-service chatbot of a major airline provided hallucinated information to a passenger on how to obtain a refund. The airline refused to proceed with the refund citing that the actual conditions were different from what the chatbot had indicated. A court ordered the company to honor the refund anyway, saying that the airline "does not explain why customers should have to double-check information found in one part of its website on another part of its website." The story made headlines, and the airline disabled the chatbot soon after (see https://mng.bz/galG).

The industry of self-driving cars has perhaps been the greatest casualty of AI's hallucinations. Once a booming industry, now it is flailing, and its future is uncertain. One of the main reasons is that self-driving cars keep making surprisingly bad decisions due to hallucinations, especially in uncommon situations that aren't present in the training data.

Hallucinations can kill a product

For example, in October 2023, a self-driving car hit a pedestrian in California right after she'd been hit by another car. The pedestrian was visible in the camera's sensors, yet the AI didn't classify her correctly. An engineering firm explained, "The pedestrian's feet and lower legs were visible in the wide-angle left side camera from the time of impact to the final stop, but, despite briefly detecting the legs, neither the pedestrian nor her legs were classified or tracked by the vehicle" (see https://mng.bz/eyAq). Instead of stopping, the self-driving car continued driving, dragging the pedestrian 20 feet.

The car in question had been manufactured by Cruise, one of the foremost self-driving car companies and a subsidiary of General Motors. After the incident, Cruise had its license to operate in California revoked, and the company decided to recall all its vehicles in the United States.

A month after the incident, it was revealed that Cruise cars weren't actually driving themselves as much as it appeared. Instead, humans had to remotely intervene every 2.5 to 5 miles to assist the vehicles (see https://mng.bz/pKlw).

A few months later, Waymo, which is Google's self-driving car initiative, was involved in a similar scandal. A Waymo car hit a truck that was being towed in an unusual way. A few minutes later, another Waymo car hit the same truck. Waymo explained (https://mng.bz/OBga),

A Waymo vehicle made contact with a backwards-facing pickup truck being improperly towed ahead of the Waymo vehicle such that the pickup truck was persistently angled across a center turn lane and a traffic lane . . . and a few minutes later another Waymo vehicle made contact with the same pickup truck while it was being towed in the same manner. . . . We determined that due to the persistent orientation mismatch of the towed pickup truck and tow truck combination, the Waymo autonomous vehicle incorrectly predicted the future motion of the towed vehicle.

As we can see from Waymo's explanation, the manufacturers attribute the problem to the truck being towed in an unusual way, which made AI not recognize the truck as such. This is an example of AI not coping with an edge case.

As is often the case with hallucinations, Waymo engineers took action to patch this specific problem with ad hoc actions. Waymo explained, "After developing, rigorously testing, and validating a fix, on December 20, 2023, we began deploying a software update to our fleet to address this issue." But what about other unusual problems Waymo cars haven't been specifically patched to deal with? What if a truck is painted with an unusual color or a pedestrian is wearing an unusual wig?

Applying patch after patch doesn't seem to be working well for the industry, as problems persist, and some companies are giving up. A Bloomberg article declared, "Even after $100 billion, self-driving cars are going nowhere" (https://mng.bz/YDja). Uber, Lyft, Ford, and Volkswagen have all abandoned their self-driving initiatives. The remaining contenders, Cruise and Waymo being among the most important ones, keep moving their goalposts. Unless we discover a new AI methodology that doesn't hallucinate, they'll probably have to keep moving them.

Living with hallucinations

Because hallucinations might remain part of AI for quite some time, it's best to learn how to live with them. We should keep them in mind from the very start when we use AI or build an AI-related product. In chapter 4, we'll discuss that there are many AI applications in which hallucinations aren't a big problem, so we have the highest chances of building a successful AI product. In other cases, in which hallucinations matter, we should assess their effects and think of mitigation and detection strategies early on.

Summary

- Hallucinations are confidently wrong outputs generated by AI.
- Common types of hallucinations are made-up facts, misinterpreted information, and incorrect solutions to problems.

Summary

- One cause of hallucinations is that AI's internal world model is insufficient to describe how our world operates.
- Another cause is that AI models are often trained to do one thing and used for something else—they're misaligned with our goals.
- Hallucinations are not going away anytime soon because this would require modifying prevailing machine learning methods in a yet-unknown way.
- Hallucinations are sometimes unacceptable or unsafe for users, which can deeply hurt a product's chances of success.
- Hallucinations can be mitigated by using prompt engineering techniques, and they can be detected sometimes.
- We must keep hallucinations in mind throughout the life cycle of an AI-related product.

Selecting and evaluating AI tools

This chapter covers

- Distinctions among different types of AI, or ways of using AI, and how to select the most appropriate one
- How to assess AI's performance and select models
- Common ways to measure AI's performance at a task

This chapter provides guidance on selecting an AI model or tool and assessing its performance at a given task. We kick off by discussing three common distinctions between different types of AI: proprietary versus open source AI, off-the-shelf versus fine-tuned AI, and AI apps versus foundation models. We explain what these mean and how to pick the most suitable type. Afterward, we discuss a common process to assess AI's performance, which uses different datasets for validation and testing. We also discuss some common performance measures such as accuracy. The appendix includes a catalog of popular generative AI tools.

Proprietary vs. open source

In proprietary AI, the user isn't allowed to modify or even see the code that powers the underlying ML models. The inner workings of the technology are kept secret to prevent others from copying it. One common way of using proprietary AI is through customer-facing apps such as ChatGPT. These tend to charge users a monthly subscription to access the service, although some provide a free tier that grants access to a reduced number of features.

Another common way of using proprietary AI is via APIs. These let users interact with AI programmatically to build apps that utilize it. The AI software runs on a remote server behind closed doors, so the user can't see the code. APIs are typically billed based on usage (e.g., the number of input and output tokens).

In contrast, in open source AI, the provider publicly discloses the internal details of the ML model, including the code to use it and the values of all the model's parameters. The user is often authorized to modify or customize the model if needed. In addition, users can self-host these models using their own infrastructure; for example, you can download a copy of the model to your local computer or your own cloud computing instance and run the code yourself. This doesn't mean you *must* self-host the model as it may also be available through APIs, but you have the option to self-host it. An example of open source AI is the family of Llama models produced by Meta, which are openly available for download on multiple websites.

Open source AI is sometimes not quite as open as it may sound. For starters, their manufacturers don't disclose the data used to train these models. So, while you can see the parameters of the final model, you'd be unable to train that exact model yourself as you wouldn't know which data to use. Mistral AI, a company that provides open source AI, explains (https://mng.bz/rKQy):

> *We do not communicate on our training datasets. We keep proprietary some intermediary assets (code and resources) required to produce both the Open-Source models and the Optimized models.*

84 *Selecting and evaluating AI tools*

> *Among others, this involves the training logic for models, and the datasets used in training.*

Note that, just like proprietary models, open source models are improved (or aligned) by using reinforcement learning with human feedback (see chapter 1). This is performed using data created manually by human labelers, which remains undisclosed in most cases.

The licenses to use open source AI often come with restrictions. For example, you are not allowed to use a Llama model—even your own copy—for an app with more than 700 million monthly users (see https://mng.bz/VVoG). In that case, you would have to discuss licensing options with Meta, and you may be asked to pay. Moreover, you're not allowed to use a Llama model or its outputs to improve other LLMs; in other words, you can't use Llama to build products that compete with it.

Building large ML models is expensive, so the most powerful open source AI is built by for-profit companies that charge or intend to charge for services. These services often include consulting or access to premium, proprietary models.

How to decide

Proprietary AI is most suitable when you need a done-for-you solution. Using proprietary AI doesn't usually require specialized knowledge, such as machine learning, coding, and DevOps.

One of the main reasons to use open source AI is to be able to self-host it (run it on your own servers), which can provide better transparency and governance, as you have full visibility over the code and full control over which data exits the organization. Your company may not want to send any sensitive data to a third party, such as OpenAI, or it may want to audit the code to ensure it doesn't do anything it's not supposed to.

The cost of self-hosting AI, however, tends to be higher than paying for APIs, as you need to maintain the required infrastructure, so it is usually not cost-effective unless done at a very large scale. You also need to be very careful—malicious open source models have been published in the past that executed unintended code in the user's machine (see https://mng.bz/xKeX).

Another reason to use open source AI is customization. If you want to modify a model (e.g., by fine-tuning it, which is covered in the next section), then open source AI lets you do so most freely. Table 3.1 summarizes the best uses of proprietary and open source AI.

Table 3.1 Proprietary vs. open source AI

Proprietary AI Best for . . .	Open source AI Best for . . .
• Done-for-you solution • Easy start • No specialized knowledge required • Small-scale use, in which pay-as-you-go AI is cheaper than maintaining your own infrastructure	• Self-hosting so that you enjoy better governance and transparency • Large-scale use, in which maintaining your own infrastructure is cheaper than pay-as-you-go AI • Model customization (e.g., fine-tuning)

In terms of the quality of outputs, proprietary AI used to hold an edge over open source AI. However, the gap has been narrowing, and many people claim that open source AI is already or will soon be as capable as its proprietary counterparts.

Off-the-shelf vs. fine-tuning

When it comes to improving the performance of generative AI at a certain task, there are two main schools of thought. One of them is using off-the-shelf models—without any alterations—and it relies on prompt engineering techniques to make them more performant and customized to your intended task. For example, it has become popular to include a few demonstrations of how to perform a task inside the prompt, which is known as *few-shot prompting* (as opposed to *zero-shot prompting* in which you don't provide any examples). This helps disambiguate the request. Researchers from OpenAI argued (https://arxiv.org/pdf/2005.14165):

> *If someone is asked to "make a table of world records for the 200m dash", this request can be ambiguous, as it may not be clear exactly what format the table should have or what should be included (and even with careful clarification, understanding precisely what is desired can be difficult).*

The researchers went on to show that including a few examples of how to perform the task within the prompt steered the LLM in the right direction.

In addition, the RAG approach (see chapter 1) has become a popular way of providing the LLM with a large amount of contextual information to help it perform a task. The increasingly large context window of state-of-the-art LLMs has made RAG particularly effective.

Improved prompts can help customize image generation. For example, the image generator Midjourney lets users upload images as part of their prompts to indicate the desired style of the generated images.

The other school of thought suggests altering the model to make it more suitable for the intended task, which is known as *fine-tuning*. The model's internal parameters are adjusted, so you utilize an altered copy of the original model to generate your outputs.

Fine-tuning requires training data, which is used to continue the training of the original model for a little longer. For example, to fine-tune an LLM, you must create a sample of text in your intended style. This data is fed to the training algorithm to refine the LLM. The amount of data used for fine-tuning is usually much smaller compared to the data used to train the original LLM—you may need just a handful of documents to do so. Open source models are ideal for fine-tuning as you have access to the entire model with its parameters, and you can then alter the parameters to better suit your needs.

Perhaps the biggest challenge of fine-tuning is overdoing it—if you specialize your model too much on your fine-tuning training data, it might end up memorizing specific examples present in the data and not perform well with other instances. This is known as *overfitting*.

There are a handful of techniques to prevent overfitting (see the sidebar). You need to be mindful of these techniques and configure the fine-tuning algorithm appropriately to prevent overfitting. We'll discuss later in this chapter how you can use validation and test sets to evaluate and compare different AI models, which can help select the best strategy to fine-tune a model and ensure the final model hasn't overfitted the data.

Techniques to control overfitting

Early stopping—You train the model on your fine-tuning data only for a few iterations. You stop once performance stops improving, as measured on a separate piece of data (called the *validation* set).

Limited scope of updates—You only allow some parts of the model to be updated. For example, one popular method called LoRA inserts small layers with new learnable parameters into the model, while keeping its original parameters intact.

Regularization—You add a term to the loss function that penalizes too high or too low parameter values. This reduces the risk of overfitting by preventing parameters from being overly specialized to specific training examples.

Dropout—Pieces of the model are randomly removed on each iteration of the training process, which prevents internal units of the model from overly specializing to the training examples.

A method known as LoRA has become popular for fine-tuning (see https://arxiv.org/abs/2106.09685). LoRA inserts small layers with new learnable parameters to adjust the existing model, instead of modifying its original parameters. This makes fine-tuning faster as few parameter updates must be calculated on each iteration. It also helps control overfitting as you only modify a limited number of parameters (see "Limited scope of updates" in the sidebar).

The libraries developed by Hugging Face are very popular for fine-tuning existing models (https://huggingface.co/docs/trl/main/en/index). Hugging Face also contains a large inventory of open source models you can fine-tune. Many users run their fine-tuning using Jupyter notebooks connected to cloud-computing instances. Google Collab is particularly commonly used for this, as it provides easy-to-access notebooks and lets you use some of its computing power for free, which might be enough to fine-tune some models.

Fine-tuning requires some specialized machine learning knowledge, so I recommend you learn the basics of ML to get it right. You might also require infrastructure to run the fine-tuning process, and you'll then have to use your own customized copy of the model.

In some cases, it is also possible to fine-tune proprietary AI. For example, OpenAI lets you upload your own fine-tuning dataset and create a fine-tuned version of its models, which you can access through the API. The company charges a premium for using fine-tuned models compared to using OpenAI's original models. The process is friendly, although not as customizable as fine-tuning open source models.

How to decide

Prompt engineering is the most straightforward way of improving a model's performance. Common advice is that it's the first thing you should try (check out https://mng.bz/AQZx and https://mng.bz/ZlQA for more info). As context windows have become large, prompts can be quite rich. So, it is often advisable to use fine-tuning as a last resort when the output still isn't quite what you expect, even after trying multiple ways of improving the prompts. Note, however, that prompt engineering works best with the most advanced and costly models, as they can adapt better to a wider range of tasks and fit longer prompts within their context windows. Table 3.2 compares off-the-shelf with fine-tuned AI.

Table 3.2 Off-the-shelf vs. fine-tuned AI

Off-the-shelf AI Best when . . .	Fine-tuned AI Best when . . .
• Prompt engineering techniques work well. • It is okay to use proprietary AI. • You can afford large models. • You prioritize ease of use.	• You want highly customized outputs, and you've exhausted other options. • You need to use smaller models (for example, for self-hosting them). • You have ML expertise and access to computing resources.

Fine-tuning can be a good choice for smaller models, for example, because you want to reduce your costs. This is particularly relevant when you must self-host your own models. In this case, using a small, fine-tuned model might be more effective than using prompt engineering with a larger model.

Customer-facing AI apps vs. foundation models

Customer-facing AI apps help final customers perform tasks. These include general-purpose commercial chatbots such as ChatGPT and special-purpose apps such as GitHub Copilot and Cursor, which help software engineers write code.

In contrast, foundation models are large, multipurpose AI models. These models are used behind the scenes to power customer-facing apps. For example, foundation models such as GPT-4o are used to power customer-facing ChatGPT.

Some companies build both customer-facing apps and provide access to their underlying foundation models through APIs so that software developers can build their own apps on top.

How to decide

Customer-facing apps are the most suitable choice when you want AI to assist you in performing a specific task, as they're friendly to use and particularly tailored to the task. Foundation models are best used as a building block when you want to

90 *Selecting and evaluating AI tools*

create your own app based on powerful AI. Table 3.3 compares customer-facing AI apps with foundation models.

Table 3.3   Customer-facing AI apps vs. foundation models

Customer-facing AI apps Suitable for . . .	Foundation models Suitable for . . .
• Assistance with a specific task	• Powering AI-based apps
• End users	• Engineers

Model validation, selection, and testing

If you want to accurately compare and select AI models, it's a good idea to build a benchmark to assess their respective performances. Also, for reasons that will become apparent soon, we often overestimate machine learning's performance, so it's good to follow a well-designed assessment process to prevent bad surprises.

This section describes the ideal protocol to evaluate AI's performance at a task. In this protocol, AI models are built and evaluated using three different collections of data, known as *datasets*. In the following, we describe the role of each type of dataset and how it should be used.

Training set

The training set is the dataset used to build the model. It contains a large collection of examples of how to perform the task. For example, for image generation, it comprises numerous images paired with captions that describe their content. For text generation, it comprises a large amount of text. A much smaller training set is also used to fine-tune a model.

During training or fine-tuning, the training algorithm tries to find model parameters that minimize the loss on the training set (see chapter 1). The loss is a mathematical function that quantifies how far off the model is from performing the required task well, such as predicting the next token in the case of LLMs.

Model validation, selection, and testing   **91**

The loss is usually designed to have nice mathematical properties, such as differentiability, so it's not always the most intuitive way of understanding a model's performance. In addition, the loss does not always quantify how good the model is at your intended task. For example, if you want to use AI to solve coding problems, the training loss does not explicitly quantify its coding abilities; instead, it quantifies how well it autocompletes text, which is only indirectly related to coding abilities.

You don't have to worry much about creating a training set unless you're fine-tuning a model or training one from scratch. However, you might need to be mindful of what data was used for training when creating the validation and test sets (more on this in a minute).

Validation set

The validation set is used to compare the performance of different models. For example, you could use a validation set to compare the performance of GPT-4o and Llama 3 at performing a task. This helps you pick the best model, which is known as *model selection*.

The performance on the validation set is usually calculated using a measure close to your actual business objective. For example, you could calculate how often the model solves coding problems correctly. Note this is often different from the loss function used for training or fine-tuning the model. There's a list of common performance measures later in this chapter.

It's important that data in the validation set is not present inside the training set. Otherwise, you might overestimate the model's performance. This is because a poor model that overfits the training data (it memorizes specific instances) may go undetected, as some of the memorized data will also appear in the validation set it's evaluated on. If the validation set is included in the training set, it's a bit like an exam that contains questions present verbatim in the textbook—students could memorize answers without genuinely learning and pass the exam.

You need to be particularly careful about this when using LLMs as they're trained on a huge amount of publicly available data that includes solutions to many problems. Suppose you want to use an LLM to help you solve crossword puzzles. You create a validation set by gathering clues from real *New York Times* crosswords published in the past. You then count how often the LLM identifies the right word based on the clues. The problem is that there are numerous websites that explicitly provide the solutions to all past *New York Times* crosswords, clue by clue. So, at least in theory, an LLM could memorize the exact solution to each past clue. Your validation data would thus assess the LLM's performance at solving problems whose solution it had the answer to. A better way of doing this would be to create a validation set containing new clues that haven't appeared in past puzzles. This way, the LLM wouldn't be able to "cheat." Alternatively, you could make sure that the puzzles in the validation set were published after the LLM's training data cut-off date.

The validation set can also be used to help you make high-level decisions when you're training or fine-tuning your own model. For example, you can train two models with different numbers of layers or different learning rates (how much the model's parameters are updated on every training iteration), and then pick the model with highest performance on the validation set. You could also use a validation set to compare different prompt engineering approaches.

Test set

Using a validation set is not enough to properly assess a model's performance. Because you're specifically selecting the model that works best on the validation set alone, you might get an overly optimistic idea of its performance. After all, you discarded the models that weren't as good on that specific piece of data. What if the selected model only works well on the validation data by chance and is not a better model in general?

So, after you're done picking the best model using the validation set, you must perform a final check using *another* dataset, called the *test set*. The test set gives you an idea of the model's performance on data that has genuinely never been used to make modeling decisions. This final assessment is a sanity check.

The test set can only be used once. If after the test you find performance disappointing and want to update the model or consider alternatives, you must collect a new test set to perform a new assessment. Otherwise, you end up using the test set repeatedly for model selection, so it turns into a validation set.

It is up to you to choose how thorough you want to be when following this process. I know of hedge funds that are very stringent about following it, as a lot of money is at stake. For example, they try not to even look at the data inside the test set to, say, plot a graph. This way, they prevent knowledge about the test data from creeping into modeling decisions, so the test data is as independent as possible.

Performance measures

This section describes some common performance measures that can be used to evaluate AI's performance at an intended task.

Accuracy

Accuracy is the percentage of tasks performed correctly. For example, 90% accuracy means that 9 out of 10 solutions are correct, as measured on the validation or test sets.

Accuracy is commonly used for classification tasks. For example, it is often used to assess how good AI is at categorizing an image or detecting a tweet's sentiment. You can also use it for other problem-solving tasks. For instance, you could use accuracy to measure an LLM's ability to solve coding problems—you'd need to count the number of correctly solved problems and divide it by the total number of problems in your validation or test set.

Precision and recall

In information retrieval, we are interested in identifying relevant instances out of a much larger pool. For example, a law firm may use a RAG approach to retrieve relevant legal cases, according to a query, from a large database of past cases. As another example, a bank may want to identify fraudulent transactions out of a (hopefully) much larger pool of transactions.

Two common performance measures are recall and precision. However, as we'll discuss in a minute, neither can be used by itself.

Recall measures how many relevant instances are identified. For example, 90% recall means that 9 out of 10 relevant instances are retrieved, the remaining being missed.

Precision measures how relevant the retrieved instances are. For example, 90% precision means that 9 out of 10 retrieved instances are truly relevant, the remaining being irrelevant or a false positive.

The challenge is that there is a tradeoff between precision and recall. Consider a system that retrieves too much stuff. For example, it could determine that almost every past legal case is relevant to every query. This system would achieve very high recall, perhaps close to 100%. However, it would be plagued with false positives, so its precision would be very low.

In contrast, consider a system that doesn't retrieve much stuff at all. For example, it may consider almost every past legal case irrelevant regardless of the query. This system would achieve close to 100% precision, but its recall would be very low.

So, to properly quantify AI's performance at information retrieval, you must somehow combine recall and precision into a single measure. A popular way to do this is to calculate the *F-measure*, which is the harmonic mean (a sort of average) between precision P and recall R:

$$F = 2(P\,R)/(P + R)$$

The higher the F-measure becomes, the higher the recall and precision. It takes its maximum value when recall and precision are both 100%.

I'm not a big fan of the F-measure for two reasons. First, it gives equal importance to recall and precision. This is arbitrary. In reality, a business may not care equally about them. I advise you to be wary of any promises of a measure that is universally good for information retrieval, be it the F-measure or something else, as the relative appetite for precision and recall is business specific.

Second, the F-measure is difficult to interpret, as the harmonic mean is not very intuitive. Technically, the F-measure is the reciprocal of the average of the reciprocals, which leads to the above formula after some algebraic manipulation. Good luck at communicating that to the business!

In my opinion, your best bet is to try to understand the business's preferences with respect to precision and recall and come up with a custom measure that considers that. In the following paragraphs, I explain one of my preferred ways of doing this.

The first step is to understand the business's minimum desirable level of recall (it can also be done with precision, but we'll use recall here). For example, the business may want to make sure to always recall at least 95% of relevant legal cases or fraudulent transactions.

Afterward, you tune the system so that it attains the desired level of recall. One way to do this is to have AI output relevance as a numerical score, with values ranging from 0 (totally irrelevant) to 1 (totally relevant). Instances above a certain relevance threshold are considered relevant. You pick the threshold that helps you attain the desired level of recall. For example, it could be that setting a threshold of, say, 0.7, above which an instance is considered relevant, helps you attain the required 95% recall (you can use the validation set to calculate the threshold).

Finally, you use the other measure—precision in this case—to report performance. You can thus compare different models (all attaining the desired recall) by how precise they are.

Mean absolute error and root mean squared error

If you use AI to make a numerical prediction, such as the amount of rainfall, you must calculate how far off predictions are from actual values. One straightforward way of doing this is to calculate the absolute difference between predicted and known values in the training or test sets and average the results. This is known as the *mean absolute error*, or MAE.

An alternative is to square the differences, which makes them all positive, average the results, and then take the square root of this number to (sort of) undo the effect of squaring. This is known as the *root mean squared error*, or RMSE. This measure is quite popular owing to its nice mathematical properties (in particular, its differentiability) and because it penalizes larger deviations more due to the squaring of the difference. However, it's not as easy to interpret as MAE.

Summary

- Proprietary AI is a good choice when you need an easy-to-use, done-for-you solution.

- Open source AI is a good choice when you need to self-host or customize models.

- If AI isn't working quite the way you expect, or you need to customize it, it's usually recommended to still use off-the-shelf models and enhance your prompts. If that doesn't work, you may want to fine-tune a model to your own data. Fine-tuning is also a good option when you prefer to use a smaller model.

- Customer-facing AI apps are designed to be friendly and useful to end users. They're powered by foundation models behind the scenes, which are large, general-purpose AI models you can use to build your own AI-based apps.

- Make sure to use a validation set (with data not present in the training set) to compare and select models. You should also perform a sanity check afterward using a separate test set, once you've selected your favorite model. Do not use the test set twice.

Summary

- The accuracy of a model measures how often it performs a task correctly. Measures such as precision and recall are used for information retrieval (e.g., fetching relevant legal cases according to a query from a much larger pool of legal cases). Precision and recall cannot be used by themselves; they must be combined in a way that matches business preferences about their relative importance. You can use the mean absolute error (MAE) or the root mean squared error (RMSE) to evaluate the performance of a model at predicting a number (such as the amount of rainfall).

When to use (and not to use) AI

This chapter covers

- Questions that can help you decide whether to build a certain AI-based product
- Questions that can help you decide whether to use conversational AI as an assistant for a certain task and the challenges that may arise
- Caveats before writing software as an LLM wrapper so that an LLM does the heavy-duty work under the hood

This chapter includes a short checklist to use when determining whether AI will work well for you. The list contains seven questions, which I hope can help you unveil the challenges and opportunities of using AI. The first three questions are framed within the context of building an AI-based, production-level product, such as a travel-planning app based on a large language model (LLM). I hope these questions will help you determine whether a certain AI-based product could be successful before building it.

The following three questions are framed within the context of using conversational AI in daily work, such as an LLM to help you code. I hope they will help you figure out whether AI is a valuable addition to your workflow.

Finally, the last question concerns the new practice of building apps in the form of LLM wrappers, in which an LLM does the job under the hood, and the app manages the LLM. This question is intended to help you determine whether this approach will be suitable for your needs.

Building an AI-based product

This section contains three questions to be kept in mind when building an AI-based product. The first question is business related. It might seem odd to think about business when deciding whether to use AI. However, in my experience, the failure to do so leads to many unsuccessful AI projects. So, I think that wondering whether there's a business case for AI is a good place to start. The other two questions are technical.

Am I putting AI before the customer?

An employee of a startup reached out to me once for advice. His company, which built accounting software, was looking to add a ChatGPT-based feature to its app, but they didn't know what that could be. He asked me if I could help him come up with possible features based on ChatGPT that they could add. I asked him why he wanted a ChatGPT-based feature in the first place, and he explained, "We're trying to raise funding, and we cannot tell investors that we're not using ChatGPT for something."

This is how many AI-based projects start—people decide to use AI due to hype, FOMO, funding opportunities, and so on, without necessarily knowing what they will use AI for. They have a hammer, and they're searching for nails.

The problem with this approach is that you often end up building products that people don't really need. A stellar example is the fancy AI-powered supermarket checkout technology developed by Amazon. This technology, called "Just Walk Out," was meant to use AI to analyze videos and automatically prepare shoppers' receipts—the shoppers didn't need to visit a checkout counter.

Amazon first developed a similar technology for its own warehouses, which helped track items picked by workers from shelves. After developing this technology, Amazon wondered what else it could do. The company had a hammer, and it started searching for nails.

The nail they came up with was the supermarket checkout process. Instead of responding to an actual shopper need, Amazon pushed this technology into grocery shopping, as if the technology by itself would be appealing enough. Here's an excerpt from my book, *Siliconned* (Applied Maths, 2024), where I discussed the problem:

> *The reception of the shops by the public was lukewarm. It appeared that people didn't care as much about fancy checkout technology as they cared about finding the best shopping deals. A business consultant explained, "Retailers must also provide competitive pricing and an enjoyable customer experience. Just Walk Out isn't enough." ... I always struggled to understand what problem Amazon was trying to solve for shoppers. Were shoppers really that annoyed about checkouts that they'd flock to Amazon Go shops just to avoid it? ... If it was about reducing the cost of operating a supermarket and thus offer better deals, it was also unclear how the technology would accomplish that, as supermarkets with the Just Walk Out technology required as many employees to run as regular supermarkets with self-checkout machines, plus the cost of installing and running the complicated technology.*

As this technology didn't seem to meet real needs, Amazon ended up suspending its development and closing many of its shops.

The increasing popularity of AI has led many people to adopt an AI-first approach, in which they try to find use cases for AI instead of first trying to understand what customers want. For example, I know a company that created a team exclusively dedicated to finding things to do with AI within the

Building an AI-based product

organization. I also know companies that hired dozens of people for newly created AI teams without knowing exactly what these teams would do with AI—they thought that, as AI seemed so promising, they would surely find something to do with it.

Another example of an AI-first approach is a large portion of the self-driving car industry. Many self-driving car companies were born because people observed that AI had become much more powerful at image categorization, thanks to convolutional neural networks. So, they thought it was the right time to develop self-driving cars, and they raised billions from investors promising big profits. In many cases, however, these startups didn't know which problem self-driving cars would solve for customers, or how they'd turn them into commercially viable products. Often, the approach was, "If you build it, they will come."

While this approach where AI is put before the needs of customers might work sometimes, it goes against prevailing wisdom in the fields of entrepreneurship and innovation. These fields have increasingly adopted a customer-centric approach. For example, the popular *lean* movement suggests one should build a minimal product early on—perhaps a prototype or a mock-up—to show to customers and learn about their genuine needs before going all-in on a solution.

Venture capitalist Itamar Novick argues (https://mng.bz/ DMrV):

> *"If you build it, they will come" is the anti-pattern where startups make decisions based on their vision of how a solution should look, ignoring or underemphasizing customer needs and neglecting to collect sufficient product validation from prospective customers.*
>
> *The origin of this anti-pattern is the allure of "a great idea." Entrepreneurs, driven by their passion and conviction, tend to assume that their product's brilliance alone will captivate customers and guarantee success.*
>
> *Unfortunately, the mere existence of a product doesn't automatically translate into customers flocking to buy it. The "if you build it, they will come" mentality often leads to a lack of product-market fit, a leading cause of early-stage startup failure.*

102 *When to use (and not to use) AI*

Unless you work in pure research or other noncommercial pursuits, my advice is to adopt an entrepreneurship mindset. Try to ensure you understand your customers and find the best solution to their problems—it may or may not be AI. For example, if you're asked to build an AI-based product because AI is trendy, if possible, go back to the drawing board to understand what the real need is and whether an AI-based product is the best way to address it.

If you can, ask yourself whether you are considering your customers' needs, or you are simply trying to find a nail to hammer with AI. If the answer is that you're putting AI before your customer needs, chances are that the project will not make it off the ground. If you are planning to use AI in response to a genuine customer need, then we can check off the first point on our list (see table 4.1 at the end of this section). This is an indicator that AI may be a good solution for you.

Are hallucinations okay?

In some applications, hallucinations aren't a big deal. An example is the translation of hotel reviews on websites such as Booking.com or Tripadvisor, which are done by AI. Travelers prefer to see as many reviews as possible, even if some are incorrect, so hallucinations aren't a big deal.

In other applications, hallucinations are not quite acceptable. We've covered many examples of that in this book already. Just in case, here's another example explained in *The Economist* (https://mng.bz/lY5o):

> McDonald's, a fast-food chain, recently canned a trial that used AI to take customers' drive-through orders after the system started making errors, such as adding $222-worth of chicken nuggets to one diner's bill.

Before using AI, I recommend that you ask yourself whether hallucinations would be a big deal. Maybe they wouldn't be as in the example of hotel reviews, so using AI would be just fine. In other cases, hallucinations might be a problem, as in the McDonalds story. In this case, you'll have to decide whether

Building an AI-based product   103

using AI is such a good idea in the first place, as it might end up killing the product if customers find it unacceptable. Or, perhaps, you might be able to reformulate the task in a way that makes hallucinations more acceptable.

For example, suppose you're building a tool to proofread legal contracts. If you frame it as a tool to "automatically correct contracts," it may lead to much disappointment (and potentially disaster) for users when it sometimes hallucinates. If, however, you frame it as "run your contract through this tool to help you find mistakes that you may have overlooked," then hallucinations might be okay, as users will now understand that it's just a tool to double-check the contract and perhaps discover unnoticed mistakes.

This brings us to the end of our second item on the checklist. If hallucinations might cause major problems, you may want to look at other solutions. If hallucinations aren't a big deal, or you can frame your AI solution so that they aren't, then you can check another point off the list.

Do I need to explain how the output is generated?

Companies love using machine learning to make predictions about all sorts of things, such as whether a client will buy a product or an industrial machine will need replacement soon. This is usually done by training a machine learning model on historical data. The richest and most complex types of models often yield the highest predictive performance.

But clients are sometimes very sensitive when it comes to understanding how predictions are generated. In some cases, this is because they don't want to take a leap of faith and trust the model, even if a metric shows that it's accurate. In other cases, they want to understand predictions to derive more insights from the model. For example, they may want to understand *why* a product is likely to be bought.

The more complex an ML model is, the more it turns into a black box and the harder it is to explain how its outputs are generated. So, the most accurate models are sometimes not appreciated much by clients who want to understand the outputs. This problem becomes even more pronounced when using deep learning models, including LLMs and CNNs, which contain many layers of processing and millions or billions of parameters.

So, before using AI, I recommend that you try to find out how much your client requires *explainability*. If explainability isn't important, then using the most advanced AI models might be the best choice, and you can check this item off the list. However, if you need explainable outputs, you might have to use a simpler model, such as a linear one, even if its performance is worse. Or you may want to formulate the problem differently, such as conducting an analytical or statistical study instead of building a predictive model.

Alternatively, if you still want to use a complex model, you may want to try to use a technique to explain some aspects of how it works. There's a whole field of study called *explainable AI* or just XAI. Many of these techniques, such as a popular one called SHAP (https://shap.readthedocs.io/), work by identifying which inputs are the ones the model relies on the most to generate its output. While these techniques reveal aspects of how ML models work, they don't provide a full explanation of how outputs are generated, so they might be underwhelming in some cases.

Researchers are now studying specific techniques to explain LLMs' outputs. For example, they have developed methods to analyze attention scores inside transformers (https://arxiv.org/abs/2401.12874). It's still very early days though. We still have no solid understanding of how large ML models produce outputs.

I wrap up this section with table 4.1, which sums up the questions we've asked so far, along with potential answers and their associated implications.

Using conversational AI as an assistant 105

Table 4.1 Checklist for building an AI-based product.

Question	Comments
Am I putting AI before the customer?	If not (you're using AI to respond to a known customer need), you're good to go.
	If yes (you're using AI as a hammer and searching for nails), you may want to take a step back and try to make sure you understand your customer's needs. You can decide afterward whether AI is a good solution to tackle them.
Are hallucinations okay?	If yes (customers tolerate hallucinations), you're good to go.
	If not (hallucinations are a big deal), you may need to reframe the problem in a way that makes them less of a big deal, or you may need to reconsider using AI in the first place.
Do I need to explain how the output is generated?	If not (customers don't need explainable outputs), you're good to go.
	If yes (explainability is needed), you may need to consider a simpler, more explainable solution instead of using the most advanced AI. Or you could evaluate whether a technique to provide some explainability to AI, such as SHAP values, would be acceptable.

Using conversational AI as an assistant

In this section, we formulate three questions that can help you decide whether to use AI as an assistant to help you perform a task. We focus on conversational AI, meaning that you describe your task as a natural-language prompt. This includes using an LLM to help you code, or using a text-to-image app to create a logo.

Can I describe the task succinctly and validate the output easily?

Conversational AI is most useful when you get "good bang for your prompt," meaning that you obtain a useful output

When to use (and not to use) AI

without having to go to great lengths to write a detailed, step-by-step prompt. So, before using it, I suggest you ask yourself:

- Can I describe the task succinctly?
- Can I validate the output easily?

For example, when writing code, there are tasks that can be described using very brief prompts such as

- Summarize what the code in this file does.
- Write a function to download a file from an S3 bucket.
- Rewrite this function in JavaScript.
- Is there a way to optimize this code?

Other tasks are much more difficult to describe as they require a detailed, step-by-step specification of the solution. In these cases, writing the prompt might be as cumbersome as writing the code itself. For example, I once had to use a library called GraphHopper, which contains algorithms to find the shortest route between landmarks in a map, but I had to customize it to measure distances in a nonstandard way. For that, we had to use a custom formula we had designed together with the client. The requirements were so specific and custom, that I'm not sure I would have saved any time by writing a prompt and having an LLM write the code. So, if your answer to the question "Can I describe the task succinctly?" is yes, there are higher chances that AI will help you solve the problem (see table 4.2 at the end of this section). As AI hallucinates sometimes, it's also important that you ask yourself the second question, "Can I validate the output easily?", especially if you're sensitive about the correctness of the output (see section 4.1.2).

Some tasks can be validated easily. For example, if you already know how to perform the task, and all you want is to save time, you can rely on your expertise to quickly validate AI's output. For example, I often forget how to use the Boto3 library to read files from S3. So, I often ask ChatGPT how to do it. Because I've already done it before and it just involves a couple of lines of code, I can easily look at ChatGPT's code and

Using conversational AI as an assistant

verify that it's correct. I can also quickly run the code to see if it fetches the required S3 file correctly.

To cite another example, if you ask an LLM whether a piece of code can be optimized, you can easily check whether its recommendations make sense to you, especially if you have coding experience and have studied things such as computational complexity. Or if you ask ChatGPT to rewrite a piece of code in another programming language, you can also verify the output if you're familiar with the target language.

In other cases, validating AI's output is not as quick or easy. For example, suppose you ask ChatGPT to write a SQL query that requires plenty of joins and business logic. Understanding the resulting query step by step may be cumbersome and take as much time as writing the query yourself. Or, if you ask ChatGPT to write code in a language you don't know, you might have a hard time debugging it.

So, if your answer to the second question—"Can I validate the output easily?"—is also yes, then AI may provide good assistance.

Has anyone done it before?

A software engineer commented on Twitter, "I sometimes wonder if coding is going to end up a bit like this" (https://mng .bz/BXr2), and shared a screenshot of the following code:

```
import ai from 'ai-thing';
const Select = ai.gen`
  A select dropdown with these options:

  - Podcast
  - Book
  - Movie


Animate the dropdown to slide down from the top
of the page in a distracting manner.
`;
```

This would be really impressive if the only tools available for frontend development were plain JavaScript, CSS, and HTML.

108 *When to use (and not to use) AI*

But that's not how most people code nowadays. We use libraries and frameworks that help us do the job. For example, I often use Material UI for frontend development, which is a collection of ready-made and visually appealing components. This is how I would create the required animated dropdown using Material UI:

```
import { Select, MenuItem } from '@mui/material';
const Select =
<Select>
  <MenuItem>Podcast</MenuItem>
  <MenuItem>Book</MenuItem>
  <MenuItem>Movie</MenuItem>
</Select>
```

This code is almost exactly the same as the natural-language description from the previous code snippet. Although this code is written using a more structured language, it is as compact and easily readable. The gains from employing AI are minimal.

So, before using an AI assistant, I recommend you wonder if some other people may have done the job before, for example, by putting together a library that does what you need. If the task is very common—a select dropdown certainly is—it's likely there's a tool out there that does it for you. These tools are often very easy to use, mature, and well tested by an active community of developers. So, they help build software quickly and robustly.

A few weeks ago, I had to write code to calculate the position of the sun in the sky at a certain time and location. Instead of wrangling trigonometric equations or asking an AI assistant how to do it, my first instinct was to search for a library for the task. I thought, "This is such a cookie-cutter task that someone must have done it before." I Googled "sun position calculation library python" and immediately found a library to do that specific job (and there are others, too). I installed it easily with just one command:

```
pip install suncalc
```

Using conversational AI as an assistant   109

The library is minimal, and its documentation is brief. You can quickly learn that it's used as follows given a datetime, longitude, and latitude:

```
from suncalc import get_position
get_position(datetime, longitude, latitude)
```

This returns exactly what I needed:

```
{'azimuth': -0.014045295626482863, 'altitude':
0.8562684198030407}
```

A few days after I'd done this, out of curiosity, I asked GPT-4o, "Write a Python function to calculate the sun position given a location and time." The chatbot wrote a complicated algorithm, with 40 lines of code. Here's a snippet:

```
n = julian_day - 2451545.0  # Days since J2000.0
        mean_longitude = (280.46 + 0.9856474 * n) % 360
        mean_anomaly = (357.528 + 0.9856003 * n) % 360
        ecliptic_longitude = (mean_longitude + 1.915
            *math.sin(math.radians(mean_anomaly)) +
            0.020 * math.sin(math.radians(2 * mean_
anomaly))))
        obliquity = 23.439 - 0.0000004 * n
        declination = (math.degrees(math.asin(math.sin(
            math.radians(obliquity)) *
            math.sin(math.radians(ecliptic_
longitude)))))
```

The algorithm was difficult to follow and contained lots of unexplained constants. Luckily, the chatbot also suggested that, as an alternative, "We can use a Python library like Astral or Pysolar." So, as a follow-up prompt, I asked, "How can I use the Astral library to do this instead?" It responded with a much shorter snippet of code, showing me how to use the library. However, I tried the code, and it didn't run, as it hallucinated the correct way to use the said library. (You can find a record of the conversation at https://mng.bz/dXGw.)

Perhaps running the prompt again or refining it would have yielded better results. My point, however, is that sometimes you're better off by finding out whether someone has already

110 *When to use (and not to use) AI*

built a tool for it. A quick Google search and scan of the documentation might be more effective than using AI, and the result may be more reliable.

So, try to ask yourself, especially if you're performing a cookie-cutter task, whether someone else may have done it before. The most effective software developers avoid reinventing the wheel and try to build on other people's proven work.

What does an excellent job look like?

One of my friends has a very interesting life story—he went from having little money and living in a hostel in exchange for a bed, to running a successful online business. A magazine wanted to share his story and asked him to write an article about it. He wrote it using ChatGPT.

He then shared the draft of the article with me and asked for my opinion. The grammar and style were pristine as expected. However, the article didn't do justice to his story. For example, it went too fast over things readers would want to know more about. Notably, it didn't say how he'd come up with his business idea while living in the hostel; instead, it jumped straight to how he'd started building the business. In addition, there were a few digressions, such as a personal opinion on a political matter, which distracted the reader from the main purpose of the article. The words were put together nicely, but the writing wasn't good because it didn't tell the story effectively. Had he submitted the story like that, in my opinion, it would have been acceptable but not the kind of thing that people read all the way through the end and recommend to others.

I gave my friend a list of comments about the article. My comments were mostly high level. For example, I advised him to slow down and tell the story in more detail sometimes, and I advised him to remove certain slow passages and digressions. I also advised him to reorganize some parts of the article that intertwined different topics.

When he read my comments, he said he'd finally understood why writing took me so much time. He also said he finally

Using conversational AI as an assistant **111**

understood why I spent money on hiring human editors. Until then, he'd thought writing was mostly about grammar. He hadn't realized how much the pacing and organization of an article could matter to make it compelling to the audience. I didn't know that either when I started writing.

It's very easy to jump to conclusions and think AI can perform a task well when we don't know much about it. We may miss important things required to do the job well and unknowingly do subpar work.

So, before using AI, I recommend you investigate what it takes to do the intended job competently. Perhaps it involves many more things than is apparent at first sight. Afterward, once you understand the job better, you can decide whether AI will do a job good enough for what you need.

Consider the task of logo design. Some companies spend a fortune on hiring top-notch logo designers. But now that AI can create logos, is it worth hiring an expensive human logo designer? Well, it depends. If you speak with a high-end logo designer, you'll discover that they perform thorough research about competitors' logos and the sentiment they convey. Afterward, they design a logo that is truly original and not a rehash of previous logos—something AI isn't great at—but at the same time somehow matches the style of competitors' logos. This helps customers quickly get an idea of what the brand is about as they recognize the type of logo from competitors, while still giving your company's logo a distinctive look.

Depending on your requirements, you may or may not need the thoroughness of high-end logo design. For example, if you're launching a startup, all you may need is a logo to fill in the space on your website as it may be too early to spend money on a higher-end design. Once the company grows and starts having repeat customers, you may want to hire a specialist to design a logo that will better position your company in the competitive landscape. Before we move on to the next section, you'll find a summary of questions and possible answers, plus their implications in table 4.2.

When to use (and not to use) AI

Table 4.2 Checklist for using conversational AI as an assistant

Question	Comments
Can I describe the task succinctly and validate the outputs easily?	If yes, an AI assistant, such as a code-writing LLM, might save you time and effort as you'd be getting "good bang for prompt."
	If not (the task is difficult to describe or validating the output is cumbersome), then you may be better off doing the job manually without AI's help.
Has anyone done it before?	If yes (for example, you're solving a cookie-cutter software task, and there's a library that does just what you need), it might be easier and more reliable to reuse other people's proven work and tools instead of asking AI for help.
	If not (your task is not very common, and it's unlikely other people's past work will help), then using AI as an assistant might be helpful to do the custom work you need.
What does an excellent job look like?	If you're familiar with what it means to do an excellent job at the required task, you're in a good position to determine whether AI can do the job satisfactorily.
	If you don't know what doing an excellent job means, you might be missing something and overestimate AI's performance. In this case, it's best if you do some research about the task to make a more informed decision about using AI for it.

Building LLM wrappers

As LLMs can tackle so many tasks, it is now tempting to build software products in a new way: Your code transforms the task into a natural-language prompt and makes an LLM do it. For example, if your app must show a list of nearby restaurants to the user based on their location, your code automatically crafts a prompt such as, "Create an HTML table listing the five restaurants closest to [the user coordinates are inserted here]. Each row should represent a restaurant, and the columns should be: The restaurant name, the cuisine style…" Afterward, your app

Building LLM wrappers

uses an LLM to perform the task, and it parses the LLM's output before displaying the restaurants to the user.

When coding this way, apps become sophisticated LLM wrappers—they manage the LLM, which is in charge of doing the heavy-duty work under the hood. I've met many early-stage startups that built or tried to build their initial products this way. They thought it wasn't necessary to code the core functionality of their apps when you could just craft a prompt and have an LLM do the work instead.

Creating LLM wrappers may be a good way of building software in some cases. In other cases, however, it's not the best solution. This section formulates one single question it may be worth asking yourself before you decide to build software that way.

Will users interact with my product using natural language?

I know a startup that was building a travel-planning app. The user would input travel details in a structured format by selecting the dates on a calendar and the destination from a list. The tool would then produce a structured sightseeing itinerary displayed in a timeline and a map. Note that this wasn't a chatbot—the user didn't converse with the app at any point by writing or reading free-form text.

Due to the popularization of LLMs, the company decided to build this feature using an LLM under the hood. The user's request was first transformed into a natural-language prompt, such as, "Create a day-by-day itinerary to visit Paris from July 1st to July 7th…" The overall prompt was lengthy, as it contained instructions on how to output the itinerary in a specific format so it could be easily parsed and rendered in the app.

The startup struggled to make this work. One of the reasons was that the LLM's output often included outdated information, such as a suggestion to visit an attraction that didn't exist anymore or at a time during which it was closed. Moreover, the LLM's output sometimes didn't fully respect the required structure. For example, it would sometimes indicate an attraction's street address where its web address should be. In addition,

114   *When to use (and not to use) AI*

it all took over a minute to run, which is too long by today's browsing standards.

The startup then realized that the problem it was trying to solve wasn't related to natural language in any way—the user didn't type in the inputs as free-form text ("I'd like to visit Paris") and the outputs weren't shown to the user as text either. So why use LLMs at all?

The startup ended up solving the problem differently: after the user made a query, the software searched for relevant attractions in the required destination using the Google Places API, which provides up-to-date and structured information about attractions, such as opening hours and coordinates. Afterward, the software ran a pathfinding algorithm to create an ideal sightseeing itinerary from those attractions. The solution ran much faster and solved the problem better.

If users will interact with your product through natural language, using an LLM might be the best choice (see table 4.3 at the end of this section), as LLMs are specially designed to process and produce natural language. For example, if you're building a customer-service chatbot, then using LLMs may be the best choice because they're designed to process written, free-form requests and generate convincing prose. In this case, you exploit what LLMs are best at.

When users will not interact with your product using natural language, such as in the travel app, you may want to think twice before using an LLM to solve it. If you use an LLM, you may not enjoy its benefits, and you'll have to cope with its drawbacks, such as long execution time, hallucinations, and unstructured outputs. In those cases, old-school software, such as a database look up, may do a better job. So, if your task does not involve natural language, analyze first whether other tools could be more suitable for the job before building an LLM wrapper.

This brings us to the end of the chapter. We've covered a few scenarios of when to use AI. I hope it will prove useful the next time you're working on a problem and wondering whether it's worthwhile to bring in an AI model.

Summary   **115**

Table 4.3 Checklist for building LLM wrappers

Question	Comments
Does my problem involve natural language?	If yes, LLMs may be a great choice, as they're specially designed to read and generate natural language.
	If not, you may want to consider alternative, old-school ways of building your software, which might be more suited to the job than LLMs.

Summary

- Adopt an entrepreneurship mindset: ensure you understand the customer's problem and find the best way to solve it, which may or may not be AI. Try not to decide you'll use AI before knowing what you'll use it for.
- Evaluate whether hallucinations are OK for your users. In some cases, such as the translation of hotel reviews, users are not too fussy about them. If hallucinations are a deal breaker, you may need to rethink the task.
- If your client wants to understand how AI generates its outputs, you may find yourself in quite a pickle, as the most powerful AI cannot be understood in detail. You might need to use a less performant but more explainable model or a technique to try to explain some aspects of the model such as the finding the relative importance of input features.
- If you use AI as an assistant, you can quickly ask yourself, "Can I easily describe the task and validate the output?" If so, you get good bang for your prompt, which is when AI is most effective. If you can't describe the task succinctly or it takes a lot of effort to validate the output, using AI may not be very useful.
- When using AI as an assistant, make sure you're not trying to reinvent the wheel. If you're performing a common

task, perhaps there's a well-documented and proven way of doing the job. For example, when coding a certain task, an open source software may already exist that will do exactly what you need, and it might be easier and more reliable to use it instead of trying to do the same using an AI assistant.

- Before having AI do a certain job, try to understand what doing that job in an excellent way entails. It might be more complicated than it seems. You can then decide whether an AI assistant will help you do the job to a satisfactory level, depending on your needs.

- Some people are building apps that are LLM wrappers—the job is done by an LLM under the hood, which is managed by the app. This is most powerful when you're dealing with a natural-language problem, either because the user inputs free-form text or the system must generate human-readable text. If your problem doesn't involve natural language, maybe using old-school algorithms instead of building LLM wrappers will be a better choice.

How AI will affect jobs and how to stay ahead

This chapter covers

- The qualities that will help protect jobs from being replaced by AI
- How software engineers can future-proof their jobs
- How AI can generate new opportunities for software engineers
- Discussing the effects of AI on the economy and whether it could prolong unemployment and misery

Because generative AI can write code, many software engineers—and aspiring ones—have become worried that their careers might be in danger. NVIDIA's CEO argued it's no longer necessary to encourage young people to learn how to code. "In fact, it's almost exactly the opposite," he said. "It is our job to create computing technologies that nobody has to program and that the programming language is human: everybody in the world is now a programmer—that is the miracle" (https://mng.bz/GenJ).

This chapter discusses the possibility that AI may replace the jobs of software engineers and how to protect such jobs. The first three sections discuss three qualities that will help them resist AI: a wide gap between "just fine" and excellent work; the need for stringent validation of the output; and the need for tight control over the output.

At the beginning of each section, we discuss the topic in general—outside software engineering. I hope this gives you a wider view of the AI affects jobs. At the end of each section, I relate the topic with software engineering specifically and share advice on how engineers can protect their jobs.

The remainder of the chapter is more speculatory and philosophical. We first discuss how AI could open new doors. Next, we discuss whether AI could cause prolonged mass unemployment and misery, which is something feared by many people.

Excellence gap

Some people have asked me whether I thought TV shows would soon be written by AI, thus replacing the job of screenwriters. After speaking with screenwriters, I've discovered that the job is often much more complicated than it may seem at first, or at least if you want to do it really well. Screenwriting is not so much about putting words together. Instead, it's about choosing what to say and how to say it, and some screenwriters go to great lengths to perform this task.

Consider the case of the spy show *Homeland*. One of the reasons the show was so popular was that every season spoke about things that were taking place in the world as it aired. As the show was shot months before it aired, the writers had to try to anticipate the things that would be relevant much later.

For this reason, the writers and crew met intelligence experts to discuss potential storylines for the following year's season. An article in *The Guardian* (https://mng.bz/zZRA) explains:

> *The team began attending an annual "spy camp" . . . absorbing the accumulated insights and knowledge of current and former intelligence agents, diplomatic old hands and, one year, National Security Agency (NSA) whistleblower Edward Snowden.*
>
> *[Claire] Danes has fond memories of the spy camps. "The days were long and dense. . . . We'd meet at nine and the revolving door*

was in constant motion, depositing one story and then another. . . .
You really did get to look into a crystal ball from all these amazing
sources and get a fairly clear picture of what our reality might be like
in a year's time."

To cite another example, consider the sitcom *Friends*. After the actors rehearsed an episode for many days, it was shot in a single day in front of a live audience. When the audience did not laugh at a joke, the writers asked the audience why. Based on the answers, writers rewrote lines on the spot and asked the audience to pick their favorite alternatives through a show of hands. That's how they made sure the lines were genuinely funny.

But not all TV shows are written that carefully. Soap operas, for example, are known to be produced quickly and cheaply. In fact, multiple episodes are usually shot every week. The storylines across different soap operas are often very similar, as writers try to recycle proven ideas.

As we can see from these examples, in some jobs, there is a large gap between seeking to achieve excellence, as in *Homeland* and *Friends,* and producing content that is just fine, as in soap operas. Let's call this difference the "excellence gap" (see table 5.1).

Table 5.1   The characteristics of "just fine" and excellent work. The latter is likely to be safer from AI.

	Just fine	Excellent
Characteristics	Value in doing the job as quickly and cheaply as possible Short-term effects Rehashed previous work	Value in doing the job thoroughly Long-term effects Original work
Examples	Writing soap operas Writing SEO-driven blog articles Quick translation of an e-commerce website	Writing high-end TV shows Writing high-end newspaper opinion piece Literary translation

In the case of high-budget TV series, the creators want the show to become a legend and stand the test of time—they want to collect royalties years or even decades later. So, writing must be done very carefully, and it takes a lot of time and skill.

In the case of a soap opera, writing quickly and rehashing existing stories is all that's needed to do the job effectively. The goal of a soap opera is to provide light entertainment, and the producers rarely intend the show to be rerun.

I asked a screenwriter whether he thought the profession was threatened by AI. He told me that perhaps repetitive, formulaic writing might be affected, the kind you find in soap operas. However, in higher-profile productions, most of the work isn't about writing itself but about conducting interviews, doing research, trying out ideas with a test audience, and so on—tasks that the likes of ChatGPT are unlikely to do.

Note that the excellence gap tends to be filled with activities with a human touch, such as networking, gathering human feedback, building relationships, and so on, for which current AI methods aren't very suitable. You can sometimes detect these activities by asking someone whether their job can be easily described as a list of steps or a recipe, which can shed light on how easy it is to automate with AI or some other technique. For example, I asked that to a journalist, and she told me that she spent a lot of time trying to come up with creative story angles, and she didn't think there was a recipe for that. Moreover, a lot of her work involved building good relationships with influential people in her area, so she could reach out to them for commentary when necessary, and she didn't think there was a step-by-step recipe that described how to do that, either.

It seems that the jobs that are safest from AI are those on the excellent side of the excellence gap, such as writing higher-end TV shows. Jobs that might suffer from AI are the ones in which the worker specializes on the low end of the gap—the "just fine" part—or there isn't much of a gap to start with—there

Excellence gap

isn't a wide difference between doing it just fine and exceedingly well, the tasks being quite mechanic and easily described as a list of steps.

Consider the case of writing SEO-driven blog articles whose goal is to drive traffic to a website from Google. For example, a travel agency may want to publish several articles quickly about a travel destination to attract traffic and then sell holidays to internauts or collect commissions from affiliate links. These articles tend to be the "just fine" kind, as the goal is to pack them with relevant keywords, not to provide insightful analyses. I'm sure you've seen articles like that. They often have titles such as "20 Things to Do in Paris This Summer (2025)."

Until a couple of years ago, it was common to hire humans on platforms such as Upwork and Fiverr to write these blog articles. I now hear that many of these workers are being replaced by AI. As this job only requires "just fine" work—it doesn't need interviews, research, networking, testing audiences, and similar—AI can do it satisfactorily and faster.

Other jobs at risk are those in which there may be an excellence gap, but excellence doesn't have much market value—people are not willing to pay for excellent work because just fine is good enough. I've spoken with many professional translators over the past few months, who reached out to me due to concerns regarding their profession. Translators often go to great lengths to produce an excellent translation, which can require a lot of research and creativity. In some cases, however, clients don't care much about that excellence—they're okay with a "just fine" translation. For example, I spoke with a group of translators who specialize in translating the content of websites, such as online shops. They seemed to be the ones struggling the most due to AI advancements, as many clients didn't mind AI translations even if they were a bit flimsy. In other cases, such as literary translation, clients are much more sensitive about the quality of the work and are less likely to be ready to replace professional, human translators with AI.

Excellence gap in software engineering

I once worked on a small freelance project where I had to create a dashboard so that a company could visualize some publicly available data more easily. I had to make a few API calls to fetch the data from various sources, transform it a little bit, and plot it. Most of my time was spent coding. The job was rather mechanical, and doing it just fine was okay.

Now, consider a different piece of work I did a few years ago. I was working for a team that wrote algorithms to put together holiday packages automatically, including determining their prices. The algorithm was meant to design packages automatically and make the process more data driven, hopefully increasing revenue. We built an algorithm that looked good on paper, but we couldn't deploy it because salespeople had concerns about it. They were scared that, by changing how we put the packages together, we would disrupt our relationship with customers. Moreover, salespeople often priced holidays strategically—for example, instead of trying to make the most revenue, they charged lower-than-revenue-maximizing prices to promote a new travel destination. They were afraid our system would make them lose control over those decisions.

To reduce friction, we had a discussion with the salespeople to understand their needs, and as a result, we came up with a mathematical gimmick to insert business constraints to our algorithm. Salespeople would be able to adjust these constraints themselves, which would give them much finer control over the holiday packages generated by our tool. Only after this intervention they were happy with it, and we could deploy the system. The success of the project was not just about coding, but about understanding what salespeople wanted and finding a solution that clicked with them.

Just like in screenwriting, there is an excellence gap in many software engineering projects. In some cases, like the simple dashboard project I mentioned, just fine is okay. The tasks involved in doing these jobs can often be written down as a

Excellence gap **123**

step-by-step recipe and delegated cheaply. This is the kind of work that AI might be able to replace.

Excellent software engineering is much more than that. Rather than just writing code as asked, the goal is to help a business solve a problem, as in the case of the package holiday example. The software engineer will work closely with the business to help devise solutions to problems. For example, they will help businesspeople identify features that provide the most added value for the least effort. They will also suggest alternative solutions that the business may have not thought of.

Moreover, excellent software developers help build robust solutions that stand the test of time. This requires finding the sweet spot between future-proofing and overengineering. For example, should your software handle multiple currencies even if all your users (for now) transact in the same currency? Or should you wait until you expand internationally to add support for other currencies? These are questions you can only answer by discussing and negotiating with the business, which often requires translating technical ideas to a language nontechnical people can understand so you can collaborate.

In addition, in excellent software development, you must make important decisions to secure the software and protect data. I once worked with a company that was particularly sensitive about accidentally letting one of their clients see data that belonged to another client. Having one isolated database per client is a way to accomplish that, but it can be overkill in some cases. After discussing different possibilities with the business, we settled for having a single database with different compartments in it, or *schemas,* which provided isolation without so much added complexity. This decision required negotiating with businesspeople.

As excellent software engineering is not just about writing code but about doing business and exercising soft skills, I think it will be well placed to resist replacement by AI. When businesspeople work alongside software engineers who genuinely help them solve business problems, they're unlikely to want to automate them away.

Recommendations

My advice is that, if you want to future-proof your career, you may want to focus on working at the intersection of technology and business—try to become the person who helps businesses attain their goals using technology, not just a person who writes code. This doesn't mean you won't be writing code; it means you'll be writing the right code to help the business succeed. If you're asked to add a feature to an app that you think is the wrong one businesswise, you should speak up.

I recommend you learn about business if you haven't yet. I've found the following books particularly useful:

- *The Lean Startup by Eric Ries (Crown Currency, 2011)*—This popular book explains a modern innovation process that relies on experimentation and validation of customer needs. The author popularized the term *minimum viable product,* or MVP, which is a simple product meant to learn about customers.

- *Value Investing: From Graham to Buffett and Beyond by Bruce Greenwald et al. (Wiley Finance, 2020)*—While the book is about investing, the first half describes where the value of a company comes from. It explains, for example, what a *competitive advantage* truly is and how it adds value to a business. It also explains the importance of future growth and when growth adds value, which is particularly relevant to ambitious, high-growth start-ups.

- *The E-Myth Revisited: Why Most Small Businesses Don't Work and What to Do About It by Michael E. Gerber (Harper Business, 2004)*—This classic book helps understand why a solid business is akin to a system that runs automatically, following clearly defined processes.

- *Venture Deals: Be Smarter than Your Lawyer and Your Venture Capitalist by Brad Feld and Jason Mendelson (Wiley,*

2019)—This book is useful to understand how financing by venture capitalists works, which is one of the most common sources of financing for technology companies.

- *Value Proposition Design: How to Create Products and Services Customers Want by Alexander Osterwalder et al. (Wiley, 2014)*— One of the main causes of tech product failure is that people don't really want the product. This book describes a process to define your target customer and the added value of your solution, which can help prevent that.

Once you learn about business, I suggest you work your way toward roles that involve both technical and business skills. For example, instead of becoming a deeper specialist on one technology, such as React, you may want to try to take up responsibilities in product management or design alongside your coding work. I advise that you to steer clear of jobs where all you do is pick up a Jira ticket created by someone else and do the technical work described in it.

You may also want to prioritize working in cross-functional teams that have defined business rather than technical goals. You could, for example, work for an agency (or build your own) that partners up with startups to help them specify, build, and validate products in exchange for money and equity, as opposed to just building whatever product the client wants— no questions asked.

In addition, you could specialize in a technical field aiming to help attain business goals, such as *operations research* and *data science*. One of the main tasks of operations research is to build mathematical optimization algorithms to help solve business problems, such as finding the optimal way of allocating inventory to warehouses based on a demand forecast. This requires mapping a business goal to a mathematical goal, so you're both a business and a technical person. Moreover, as you can't efficiently optimize anything, you sometimes need to negotiate with the business to solve a simpler yet useful problem instead.

Although a bit hyped up at times, also data science sits at the intersection between technology and business, as it uses ML to help answer business questions. This is especially true of full-stack data scientists, who help all the way from ideation to building production-level data products. Occupations such as operations research and full-stack data science, in which coding and doing business are tightly coupled, may be in the strongest position to survive advances from AI.

If you're absolutely not interested in business and prefer purely technical work, you may want to specialize in a niche technology or problem area and stay up to date with developments—you could become a guru in your field. This might help you stay ahead of AI, as AI learns to code from examples of code available on the internet, which can be outdated or not abundant enough with the latest and most niche technologies.

Stringent validation

If you use hotel-booking websites such as Booking.com, you may have noticed that hotel reviews from travelers are often translated into your language. This helps you see as many reviews as possible. Instead of hiring humans to translate the reviews, these companies use AI to do so automatically. The outputs generated by AI aren't verified manually one by one. Sometimes AI hallucinates, so the translations have mistakes or sound a little funny. I just saw the following review on Booking.com: "Location perfect. Report value for money, nothing to say." The strange use of the word "report" came from the mistranslation of *rapport qualité prix* in French, which is a common way of saying "good value for money."

But travelers don't care much about these mistakes; they want to know whether a hotel is clean, well located, and so on, and they don't need a perfect translation for that. So, using AI instead of a human translator, presumably one who doesn't hallucinate, is just fine.

Another similar example is personalized recommendations on websites, such as which movie to watch next on Netflix or which product to buy on Amazon. Instead of having a marketing specialist analyze customers and create tailor-made recommendations, these are generated at scale and automatically using machine learning trained on past user data. Sometimes these recommendations aren't quite right. For example, you may be recommended to buy another washing machine after you just bought one, even though washing machines are usually a one-off purchase. But these mistakes don't matter much, as users will probably not be too fussed about poor recommendations and just ignore them.

In these cases, the correctness of the output isn't all that important. So, even though AI may sometimes hallucinate, companies might still choose it instead of hiring human workers (see table 5.2). This is often the case with "nice to have" features that aren't critical to a company's core operations, so mistakes don't matter much. It is also common with large-scale tasks that would be too time-consuming or costly to perform. For example, I think it's unlikely Booking.com would hire humans to translate all hotel reviews on its website. Between having no translated reviews and unvalidated AI-translated reviews, Booking.com chooses the latter.

Table 5.2 The characteristics of work that don't require a stringent validation of outputs. The latter is likely to be safer from AI.

	Lax validation	Stringent validation
Characteristics	Nice-to-have features Things you wouldn't do manually due to poor scalability	Mistakes can be devastating (due to legal, safety, or commercial reasons)
Examples	Translation of hotel reviews Automated product recommendations	Legal translations Verification of aircraft maintenance records Preparation of shopping receipts

128   *How AI will affect jobs and how to stay ahead*

In other cases, it is much more important to make sure that the output of a job is thoroughly validated. I recently had a conversation with the manager of a team in charge of verifying aircraft maintenance records. He explained that every time a leased aircraft switches hands between different airlines, it is imperative to make sure that all maintenance has been conducted properly. His team oversees going through all the records to verify that.

Believe it or not, all maintenance records are still held on paper—technicians fill forms manually with a pen, and piles of paper are stored in boxes (yes, in the 21st century). Each country uses different kinds of forms, and they're often filled in inconsistently, which makes the process of verifying them even more cumbersome.

A startup built a solution to automate the process using AI. However, the AI system made mistakes sometimes, and this was very difficult to correct due to scarce training data on edge cases. Because of that, a user told me they still had to go through all the papers manually to verify AI's outputs, so this app didn't end up saving much time after all. They ended up unsubscribing from the AI service and doing it all by hand as usual.

Similarly, I once met intelligence staff in the military who were thinking of using AI to identify sensitive targets in satellite images. At that time, they were inspecting the images manually by visually sweeping them using a "Z" pattern. The person in charge of the sweeping was held personally responsible for their observations, so missing a target could compromise their careers. The images covered huge areas, so this was very time-consuming.

After discussing AI with them, they soon realized it wasn't possible to guarantee that AI would identify targets with 100% accuracy. Maybe it would identify more targets than humans, but the possibility existed that it would sometimes randomly miss a target a human could see. To them, this meant they would still have to sweep the entire image manually to

Stringent validation **129**

double-check that AI hadn't missed anything. So, AI wouldn't speed up the process whatsoever.

Aircraft maintenance and military operations were examples of work that is too sensitive to leave to AI without double-checking it (see table 3.2). Other sensitive professions that require stringent validation are those of lawyers and doctors, as small mistakes can lead to lost licenses or malpractice lawsuits.

Even in other fields in which mistakes may not be as devastating, they can be harmful commercially, so humans will still be involved in validating AI's outputs manually. An example of this is Amazon's automated grocery shops. These stores, which opened in the United States and the United Kingdom, allegedly used video cameras and AI to automatically detect what a customer picked from the shelves, so logged-in users could just walk out of the store without going to the cash desk, and they received a receipt on their email later.

As is often the case, AI sometimes hallucinated, so the receipts contained mistakes. But Amazon wouldn't want those receipts to ever reach customers, as it would be very harmful for the business's reputation. So, Amazon secretly hired an army of 1,000 people who watched the videos remotely and validated AI's outputs (https://mng.bz/0Qnv). Thus, instead of eliminating the jobs of human cashiers, Amazon moved them elsewhere.

Jobs in which outputs must be thoroughly validated due to legal, safety, or commercial reasons are safer from being automated away by AI, as a human expert must still be involved in the loop. In some cases, there may be productivity gains from using AI and validating its output instead of doing the work manually. For example, perhaps AI might help draft legal contracts quickly, which lawyers will have to verify word by word (remember the unfortunate story of the lawyer who filed a document in court rife with AI hallucinations), but this two-step process will be quicker than writing the contract without AI.

In some other cases, however, the overall productivity gains will not be consequential because the validation process will be cumbersome. As illustrated by the story of aircraft maintenance records and Amazon checkouts, AI often saves much less time overall—or even makes things worse—than people initially thought.

Some professionals have told me their clients are pressuring them to use AI to work more quickly and even charge lower rates. According to the clients, now AI can do your work and you just have to validate it, so it should be faster and cheaper. For example, translators have told me that many of their clients are now asking them to be editors of AI-translated text instead of translating the text from scratch, and they want to pay less for that.

Perhaps in some professions, productivity gains will indeed be observed. However, there are some early indicators that it may not be happening as much as expected, and validation may be the culprit. A survey conducted by Upwork (https://mng.bz/KGXO) revealed that

> Nearly half (47%) of workers using AI say they have no idea how to achieve the productivity gains their employers expect. Over three in four (77%) say AI tools have decreased their productivity and added to their workload in at least one way. For example, survey respondents reported that they're spending more time reviewing or moderating AI-generated content (39%), invest more time learning to use these tools (23%), and are now being asked to do more work (21%). Forty percent of employees feel their company is asking too much of them when it comes to AI.

So, when the correctness of outputs is of paramount importance, either for safety, legal, or commercial reasons, it is unlikely that AI will completely replace human work, or at least it won't be the case as long as AI isn't 100% accurate. It might be the case, however, that some workers will find themselves being hired for lower rates to validate AI's outputs instead of generating them themselves, although the payoff of this may not always be as good as it may initially seem.

Validation in software engineering

Compared to other fields in which a small mistake can go unnoticed, software bugs are often amplified—one minor bug can break an entire application. Notably, in July 2024, a bug in an update of security software CrowdStrike caused major disruption globally, including grounding planes and disabling fire alerts in buildings. The damages are estimated to be in the billions of dollars (https://mng.bz/YD0e).

That's why software is usually validated thoroughly. Companies often ask developers to unit-test their own code and review one another's code. They also have automated tests in the deployment pipeline and separate quality assurance (QA) teams to independently validate the software.

If AI generated flawless software, then validation would perhaps no longer be necessary. But is that so?

The code generated by LLMs tends to be syntactically correct—it compiles just fine. However, it sometimes doesn't solve the intended problem correctly, or it crashes at runtime.

A software engineer performed a series of tests to understand LLMs' code-writing capabilities. In his first experiment, he asked ChatGPT to fetch publicly available data from traffic cameras in Singapore and show them on a map (https://mng.bz/jpRe). This was the prompt:

 You can get JSON data containing traffic images, camera id and location (longitude and latitude) by calling traffic images API, https://api.data.gov.sg/v1/transport/traffic-images. Show on a map (using OpenStreetMaps) where all cameras are, with the corresponding traffic image, camera id and the date and time of the image. Call the traffic images API to refresh the data and repopulate the map every 1 minute. Only use Javascript embedded within the map html file for this and nothing else.

In just one attempt, ChatGPT produced a piece of code that did exactly what it was asked to do. This was certainly impressive.

The software engineer then tried to augment the functionality of this map by also showing weather data on it:

 The 2-hour weather forecast for Singapore can be found through the Weather API, https://api.data.gov.sg/v1/environment/2-hour-weather-forecast, which returns JSON data that includes the name of the location, the longitude and latitude of the location and the weather forecast of the location in the next 2 hours. Display the information on the map that was previously returned by modifying it. Use a marker with a weather icon to indicate the weather station.

This time, ChatGPT's code didn't work correctly. After some debugging, the engineer realized it was because the LLM had assumed that the weather API returned data in a format that was not the right one. So, the engineer modified the prompt to indicate more explicitly the format of the data returned by the API. It then worked correctly.

The engineer learned from this experience and, in subsequent experiments, he made sure to write more detailed prompts to prevent ChatGPT from making wrong assumptions. Even then, the code wasn't correct all the time. For example, it persistently outputted the wrong URL to the CDN of a library.

The engineer acknowledged that ChatGPT was useful and could help you learn how to perform certain tasks. However, he argued (https://mng.bz/jpRe):

> *If you make assumptions about ChatGPT, it will make assumptions too aka hallucinate and make up stuff. The made-up stuff is just as elaborate and believable. . . . Most of the time, you'll need to debug the code, especially if you are not very specific. . . . Using ChatGPT to debug code can be enlightening or disastrous. It can be enlightening because it can give you pointers to the issue, even issues it created in the first place, and sometimes even fix it for you. It can be disastrous because it can also lead you down a rabbit hole that never ends by giving you wrong pointers and red herrings, and it will sound super-confident at every step of the way.*

As we can see from these examples and the author's reflections, we can't completely trust AI-generated code. We still

Stringent validation **133**

need to validate and debug its outputs, and the expertise of a software engineer is required to do so. In addition, the prompts that work best are the ones filled with technical details, so software engineers are the ones who can craft the most effective prompts.

That's why I find it unlikely that companies will automate away software engineers with AI-generated code. However, it may happen that some companies, persuaded by potential productivity gains, will try to turn software engineers into validators of AI-generated code. Just like in the case of translators, they may expect to pay lower rates to engineers or have them do more work, as they'd be just proofreading the AI-generated code instead of writing it. Let's see ways in which you can avoid that.

Recommendations

Let's first go over some observations and recommendations about traditional software development. I will then add recommendations regarding the validation of AI-based products.

I've heard of software development teams that dedicate most of their time to the implementation of new features, and they deprioritize testing them or leave testing for later or for others to do. While these teams produce code, they often do so unreliably. I wouldn't be surprised if business managers tried to automate them away using AI.

To protect your job, I recommend that you specialize in delivering robust software. This requires many more duties than just writing code. For example, you may spend a large and perhaps greater portion of your work making sure that your code is robust to edge cases and unfortunate situations. Even if AI can write some code for you, that is only a small portion of your duties. Your employer will see you as a person who delivers holistic and robust code that stands the test of time.

For that, I recommend joining modern software development teams that are validation driven; they intertwine development and testing and try to deliver robust software off the bat.

These teams make validation central and tightly coupled to the development process, as opposed to a secondary task.

I also recommend that you learn about *test-driven development,* or TDD, which has become extremely popular. In TDD, you divide your code into small units and spend time to think of edge cases or things that could go wrong with each unit. You then write individual tests for all these things that could go wrong, and you make sure that your code passes the tests (some people even write the tests before writing the code). I often advise others to write a test case instead every time they're tempted to run the software to see if it works well, perhaps using a "print" statement. This way, the test stays in the code base forever and can be helpful in catching problems later. But you don't want to overdo it. Part of your responsibility as a test-driven developer is to find the sweet spot between coding and testing—you shouldn't spend too much time writing outlandish tests to cover scenarios that are extremely unlikely to happen.

I also recommend you learn about *trunk-based development,* which is an increasingly popular way of organizing software teams. Before trunk-based development, each coder worked on a separate branch of the main code branch. After finishing, peers reviewed the software (in a "pull request") before it was merged into the main code. Coding and validation were thus quite separate activities.

In trunk-based development, coders directly push their updates to the main code branch without peer review (some may use short-lived feature branches). For this to work, you must adopt a set of work practices to prevent breaking the production app. For example, you may use a mechanism known as a *feature flag* to direct most users to the old version of the code and only a handful of users, such as yourself and the quality assurance team, to the new version. You only remove the old code and point every user to the new one once you validate that your new feature works as expected. Moreover, the deployment

Stringent validation **135**

pipeline must contain plenty of automated tests. You can learn more about this process on trunkbaseddevelopment.com.

When implementing modern work practices, such as TDD and trunk-based development, the job of coders is not just to write code but to help continuously deliver robust software. This involves a lot more than just writing code that implements new features, so AI may not affect it all that much.

In addition, you may want to learn how to build and deploy apps holistically, including DevOps and management of cloud infrastructure, for example. This will strengthen your position as a person who delivers robust software end to end and not just a coder, helping you stay relevant in an era when AI can write some code.

Let's now move on to AI-based products, which are all the rage. These products impose additional requirements in terms of validation, as AI sometimes hallucinates or produces different outputs on different executions. How can you properly measure the accuracy of an AI-based product in performing a task? And how can you find opportunities to improve it?

Over the past few months, many people have approached me to ask for advice about their AI-based products because they were disappointed with AI's performance. This included both developers and entrepreneurs. In addition to the odd hallucination, they often complained that AI lacked consistency. For example, a company created an AI model to generate recommendations to improve marketing videos. The users would implement one of the recommendations and then run the video again through the app, but now the app would make completely different recommendations and forget some of the previous ones. This was frustrating to users.

In most cases, I soon noticed the developers weren't following a systematic process to validate and select AI models. For example, they didn't have a benchmark to assess the performance of different models at the task or how performance improved as the prompt changed. Moreover, they summarized

How AI will affect jobs and how to stay ahead

the entire task in one single mega-prompt and hoped for the best. I encouraged them to divide the problem into smaller units and conduct thorough benchmarking. This would help diagnose the problem and identify individual subtasks that could be improved, perhaps bringing in some external data or even not using AI at all. In addition, benchmarking could help build realistic assumptions about performance and see how close you are to what's acceptable—AI will rarely work just the way you want 100% of the time. In chapter 3, we discussed the preferred process for validation and selection of models, which gives you an idea of how AI could perform in the future and avoid unfortunate biases that can arise from poor handling of the validation process.

I expect there will be an increasing need for developers to work on validating AI's performance and finding opportunities for improvement. Why not become a guru of AI-based product validation to stay ahead of the curve?

Tight control

A graphic designer told me she was trying to use AI to generate an image but was struggling to do so effectively as she couldn't get it to look *exactly* the way she wanted. As she had very specific requirements about the image, the prompt had become very detailed and long, which made it hard to manage. AI sometimes randomly ignored some instructions in the prompt, so she had to rephrase or rearrange it to try to have AI heed the requests.

The designer told me, "I must be doing something wrong. I need to read the user manual." It is true that the user manual may have provided her with some useful directions and tricks to write an effective prompt. For example, Midjourney's documentation (https://docs.midjourney.com/docs/prompts) explains:

It is better to describe what you want instead of what you don't want. If you ask for a party with "no cake," your image will probably include a cake. To ensure an object is not in the final image, try advanced prompting using the --no parameter. . . . Word choice matters. More specific synonyms work better in many circumstances. Instead of big, try tiny, huge, gigantic, enormous, or immense. . . . Plural words leave a lot to chance. Try specific numbers. "Three cats" is more specific than "cats." Collective nouns also work, "flock of birds" instead of "birds."

While these tips and tricks may have indeed helped the designer, they're still rules of thumb that don't work every time. It's unlikely that, just by following these recommendations, the designer would have easily controlled AI's output the way she wanted.

This experience is very different from that of an owner of an e-commerce website. He explained to me that he sometimes runs quick ad campaigns on Instagram to test a new product or refine its sales copy. Until a couple of years ago, he hired people to create graphics for these ads or did it himself. Now he uses AI. As he doesn't care much about the exact look of these graphics, such as the colors or images in them, he writes very simple prompts and often obtains an acceptable result in one go.

Similarly, as I write this book, the editors have been creating videos to summarize its content. They've been using AI for it. They don't need full control over the look of the videos, such as colors, design, layout, and so on. They just need to verify that the content makes sense. So, AI is very effective because a simple prompt can take you a long way.

Generative AI works best when we don't want to tightly control its output, as you can obtain useful outputs without having to refine and refine the prompt (see table 5.3). When you're not very picky about the end result, you get "good bang for your prompt."

How AI will affect jobs and how to stay ahead

Table 5.3 The characteristics of work that don't require tight control over the output. The latter is likely to be safer from AI.

	Loose control	Tight control
Characteristics	You care about core features but not finer details ("80/20" work).	You know **exactly** what you want.
	Short-lived, experimental, or add-on features.	You want the output to look a certain way, up to the finest details.
	Ready to accept AI's first output without much fuss.	Describing the task step by step can take a significant amount of time (perhaps as much as doing the job).
	No need for very detailed prompts (you get good bang for your prompt).	
Examples	Graphics for ephemeral ad campaigns.	Visual effects for high-end movie production.
	Informal videos to supplement written content.	Designs for clients with very precise requirements.

In other cases, we want to have much more control over AI's output, as we have a stronger idea of what we want to produce. In this case, generative AI may not save that much time, if any at all, as the process of precisely describing what you want in the prompt and getting AI to do it might be as complicated as doing the work manually.

So, jobs in which clients don't care much about the precise details of the output are the ones most at risk of being replaced by AI. For example, a designer who specializes in creating graphics cheaply for quick ad campaigns may need to worry. Jobs where clients have very precise requirements about outputs are the ones that may resist AI better. In these cases, AI may be of some assistance, but the worker will still have to do a lot of work to get the output as intended. For example, a visual effects artist who works for high-end movie productions, in which directors are very demanding, is more likely to resist AI.

Control in software

A few months ago, I had to quickly come up with a color palette to display lines using different colors in a line chart. The palette had to be defined as a JavaScript list of colors represented by hexadecimal strings. I asked ChatGPT the following:

give me a color palette for a graph written as a Javascript list of hex values. there should be 20 different colors

ChatGPT responded with a list of colors in the right format. Here's an excerpt:

```
const colorPalette = [
  "#FF5733", // Red-Orange
  "#33FF57", // Green
  "#3357FF", // Blue
  "#FF33A1", // Pink
  "#FF8C33", // Orange
  ...
];
```

It worked like a charm. The colors looked kind of ugly (the client said they looked jazzy), but it did the job we needed at the time, which was to visualize the data as quickly as possible. We didn't need it to look particularly well, or not just yet.

When it comes to writing code, AI is most useful when we can succinctly describe the task and don't care so much about the exact output. So, we get good bang for our prompt. Note how sloppily written my prompt was, yet ChatGPT managed to produce code I could readily use.

But not all coding tasks are like this. In fact, most often, we do care a lot about the fine details of the software we write, and stakeholders have strong opinions of how our software should tackle a problem, what its interface should look like, and so on. For example, we may need it to use a specific algorithm or a specific external API to gather data, or we way need a frontend interface to respond to different screen sizes in a specific way.

As a software project grows, it often becomes more customized and unique.

The more requirements you have about your code, the more writing an AI prompt for it becomes like coding itself, as you must define the solution step-by-step. This is one of the reasons why no-code, drag-and-drop tools to write software have never replaced programming. At one point, when you need to customize a no-code app, you end up having to either code or write step-by-step instructions using the no-code platform's capabilities, which is a lot like coding, thus defeating the purpose of no-code in the first place.

After NVIDIA's CEO argued that programming will now be done using human language, technology educator John Crickett pointed out, "How will we ever specify complex software in a language as imprecise, vague and open to interpretation as 'Human'? I've never met a product owner who has been able to do it in English. I certainly can't" (https://mng.bz/W2KW). AI might be a tool that can aid engineers, but they will still have to use precise, step-by-step technical language to define what code must do.

Recommendations

I recommend avoiding software jobs that involve building experimental products for which details don't matter much—we can think of them as toy products. One example is building quick prototypes for entrepreneurs who want to test an app idea with potential users. These clients often don't care about the scalability or future-proofing of the solution. They want you to build something quickly so they can show it to users and gather feedback. If they collect evidence that there's a real need for the product, they often throw away the initial prototype and hire engineers to build a more serious product afterward. Many of these entrepreneurs are now using no-code app builders such as Bubble or FlutterFlow, without hiring engineers, to build the apps themselves. We could imagine they'll increasingly rely on AI tools and become less inclined to hire engineers for their early-stage projects.

A new opportunity: Making the web more human

Instead, try to work on demanding projects for very picky clients. Some clients are extremely sensitive about small details and want things done in a certain way. This often derives from the demands of their own users who are perfectionists and complain about small things. You might observe this the most when building software for mission-critical applications, such as coordinating logistics operations.

A new opportunity: Making the web more human

Do you ever add the word "reddit" to your search queries on Google? I do that all the time, and it seems that there's an increasing number of people who do that, too.

For example, I recently went to the city of Belfast and wondered whether it was worth visiting Titanic Belfast, a museum built on the site where the ocean liner was built. I knew that an ordinary Google search would send me to countless SEO-driven articles with titles such as "Top 5 reasons to Visit Titanic Belfast." These articles, packed with keywords to drive traffic, would be poorly curated and filled with affiliate links to try to sell me something.

Instead, I searched "Titanic Belfast worth visiting reddit," as I wanted to know what redditors had to say on the matter. I knew opinions would differ, and perhaps redditors would fight and downvote each other, but at least I'd have a higher chance of discovering what genuine human beings thought about the museum.

Software engineer Dmitri Brereton argues, "Why are people searching Reddit specifically? The short answer is that Google search results are clearly dying. The long answer is that most of the web has become too inauthentic to trust" (https://dkb .blog/p/google-search-is-dying).

People seem to be craving more genuine, human content on the web. I think that, if AI-written content floods the web, it will make the problem even worse. People will flock to online venues where they can find more genuine content. If AI-made content proliferates on platforms such as Google,

Medium, and YouTube, they may find themselves in trouble as users flee them. Some of them, such as YouTube, have already started cracking down on AI-generated content (https://mng .bz/8OgD).

So, if you allow me some speculation, I think that the generative AI revolution may create new types of jobs to help rank and filter content based on its authenticity. For example, a new specialty may be in writing software to detect AI-generated content. This may lead to new developments and interest in the field of information retrieval.

Philosophical detour: Automation and mass unemployment

Since the rapid development of generative AI, some people have been concerned about the possibility that it would cause mass unemployment in the wider economy (https://mng.bz/ EarR). This concern isn't new—it's been voiced many times in history when machines or new techniques that automated work were introduced. As a technologist, you may often find yourself discussing the effects of your own work in the grand scheme of things—does building new technology hurt the economy?

Indeed, new machines and techniques do cause people to lose their jobs. This is very unfortunate, as workers find themselves with obsolete skills and have to search for new jobs, perhaps for lower pay. But what is the overall effect of machines on an economy—do they generate prolonged mass unemployment and widespread misery? To answer this question, let's discuss economics.

We can think of an economy as a process that takes resources and converts them into real outputs (products and services):

Resources (minerals, energy, workers' time) —> Products (e.g., food, Netflix series) and services (e.g., doctor's care, haircut).

The total output of an economy is measured by its GDP (more precisely, the GDP adjusted for inflation, or real GDP). Countries with a higher per-capita GDP produce more stuff for their inhabitants. This often means they enjoy a higher standard of

Philosophical detour: Automation and mass unemployment   143

living. The GDP of a country grows when it finds ways to produce more stuff, for example, by using more advanced production techniques or by building machines that automate away part of the manual work.

When an economy doesn't benefit from machines, many worker hours are required to produce essential items like food and clothes. When it accumulates machines, fewer hours are required to produce the same stuff, so more items can be produced, and they become cheaper.

The use of technology frees up resources, including human work hours, which can be used to innovate and produce nonessential things, such as entertainment and TV series. A 2022 study revealed that "roughly 60% of employment in 2018 is found in job titles that did not exist in 1940" (https://mng.bz/N1rd). So, while automation eliminates jobs, ultimately the economy accommodates the freed-up resources to the production of other stuff, perhaps things that weren't produced before and that aren't as essential to survive. Automation, provided that it uses resources efficiently, makes an economy richer, not poorer.

In his book *Economics in One Lesson* (Harper & Brothers, 1946), journalist Henry Hazlitt explained:

> *If it were indeed true that the introduction of labor-saving machinery is a cause of constantly mounting unemployment and misery, the logical conclusions to be drawn would be revolutionary, not only in the technical field but for our whole concept of civilization. Not only should we have to regard all further technical progress as a calamity; we should have to regard all past technical progress with equal horror. . . . Why should freight be carried from New York to Chicago by railroads when we could employ enormously more men, for example, to carry it all on their backs? . . . What machines do, to repeat, is to bring an increase in production and an increase in the standard of living.*

The conundrum is that, even if automation improves economic development overall, the transition is harsh for the people who lose their jobs in the process. Henry Hazlitt goes on to argue:

> *We should keep at least one eye on Joe Smith. He has been thrown out of a job by the new machine. . . . Now he has become overnight an unskilled workman again, and can hope, for the present, only for the wages of an unskilled workman, because the one skill he had is no longer needed. We cannot and must not forget Joe Smith. His is one of the personal tragedies . . . incident to nearly all industrial and economic progress.*

I don't think generative AI is as big a step as people claim in terms of helping us produce stuff more efficiently. As we saw, AI hallucinates and its outputs often need to be thoroughly validated. In addition, as we'll discuss later, it consumes quite a lot of electricity and other natural resources. However, it does seem to be helping perform certain tasks more efficiently in a variety of industries. This will create economic growth, not misery, in the long run, just like so many other machines have done in the past. Some people will lose their jobs in the process, and this will certainly be harsh for them. But we should not fall prey to the idea that new technology causes widespread and prolonged misery. It's quite the opposite.

Summary

- Jobs in which excellent work is noticeable and appreciated are likely to resist AI better. In software engineering, one way to achieve that is to work at the intersection between technology and businesses—you partner with businesspeople to help them build successful products, as opposed to just coding. Some suggestions to accomplish that are the following:
  - Learn about business, for example, by reading popular business books like *Lean Startup*.
  - Be involved in tasks beyond technical ones, such as product management or business analysis.
  - Specialize in a technical field designed to help businesses attain their goals, such as operations research and data science.
- Jobs requiring a stringent and detailed validation of the output, either for safety, legal, or commercial reasons, will

Summary

better resist AI. This tends to be the case with software, but some people may want to turn engineers into validators of AI-written code. Some ideas to remain relevant are

- Become a person whose job is to deliver reliable software, not just code.
- Work in modern teams that constantly intertwine coding and testing. If you haven't already, learn about modern engineering practices like test-driven development (TDD) and trunk-based development.
- Learn how to build and software holistically, including deployment, cloud, and DevOps.
- Learn good practices to evaluate AI-based products (see chapter 5). Help your clients understand the performance of AI at their intended tasks and help them find opportunities for improvements.

- Jobs that require fine control over the output may resist AI better, as AI is most helpful when you're ready to accept its outputs without having to refine them much. Some ideas to protect your job are

  - Avoid specializing in building rough prototypes or "toy products," as required by early-stage entrepreneurs for idea validation.
  - Try to work with picky clients who want things done in a certain way. You might have the highest chances of finding this kind of client when building software for mission-critical applications.

- The proliferation of generative AI may create new software jobs to build algorithms that will help cope with the newly generated content (e.g., by helping filter and retrieve content written by humans).

- Those whose professions are affected by AI will suffer through the transition to a new profession. However, if AI were to truly automate jobs efficiently, rather than cause prolonged unemployment and misery, it will make our economies more efficient and prosperous.

The fine print 6

This chapter covers

- Controversial and timely discussions around AI
- Copyright disputes regarding training data
- The economics of AI
- Exaggeration about AI's performance and advancements
- AI regulation
- Consumption of resources, such as electricity and water, to train and use AI models
- The philosophical debate around AI, biological brains, and consciousness

This chapter addresses some of the bigger questions around AI. It also reveals a less flattering AI side—how the field often suffers from exaggeration, speculation, and even deception. I think it's important to be informed about these topics, so you can analyze AI announcements and discussions critically. In addition, if you're building AI-based products or using AI intensively, you may want to be aware of the broader effects and potential controversies that could arise from your work.

Copyright

Large AI models, such as LLMs and text-to-image models, have been trained using data collected from the internet, or *scraped*, most often without authorization from its owners. This includes millions of documents, images, and books, which has made many people angry, and there have been many lawsuits against AI providers. One example is a lawsuit from Getty Images, a website that sells stock images, against Stability AI, which creates the Stable Diffusion text-to-image models. Getty Images argues that Stability AI used images collected from Getty's website without authorization to train its models. The complaint shows images generated by Stability AI's models, which are similar to those sold on Getty. In some cases, the AI model even generates images with a rough imitation of Getty Images' watermark (see figure 6.1).

Figure 6.1 Left: Image sold on Getty Images' website. Right: Image generated by a Stable Diffusion model. Note the watermark in the image. These images are reproduced from *Getty Images (US), Inc. v. Stability AI, Inc.*, 1:23-cv-00135, (D. Del.).

A similar lawsuit was filed by *The New York Times* against OpenAI on the grounds that newspaper articles were scraped without authorization to train OpenAI's models. The complaint contains examples of large portions of text outputted by GPT-4, which are verbatim reproductions of text found in *The New York Times* (see figure 6.2).

Output from GPT-4:

many of America's other global companies — aren't nearly as avid in creating American jobs as other famous companies were in their heydays.

Apple employs 43,000 people in the United States and 20,000 overseas, a small fraction of the over 400,000 American workers at General Motors in the 1950s, or the hundreds of thousands at General Electric in the 1980s. Many more people work for Apple's contractors: an additional 700,000 people engineer, build and assemble iPads, iPhones and Apple's other products. But almost none of them work in the United States. Instead, they work for foreign companies in Asia, Europe and elsewhere, at factories that almost all electronics designers rely upon to build their wares.

Actual text from *The New York Times*:

many of its high-technology peers — are not nearly as avid in creating American jobs as other famous companies were in their heydays.

Apple employs 43,000 people in the United States and 20,000 overseas, a small fraction of the over 400,000 American workers at General Motors in the 1950s, or the hundreds of thousands at General Electric in the 1980s. Many more people work for Apple's contractors: an additional 700,000 people engineer, build and assemble iPads, iPhones and Apple's other products. But almost none of them work in the United States. Instead, they work for foreign companies in Asia, Europe and elsewhere, at factories that almost all electronics designers rely upon to build their wares.

Figure 6.2   Example of GPT-4 output (almost) verbatim text as published by *The New York Times*. Figure reproduced from *The New York Times Company v. Microsoft Corporation*, 1:23-cv-11195, (S.D.N.Y.).

In addition, a group of artists sued Midjourney, Stability AI, and other image-generation providers for using images of the plaintiffs' work to train their models. They argue this allows the models to generate images "in the style of" the plaintiffs (https://mng.bz/ZlKa). It is likely that many other copyright infringement allegations will be made against AI providers in the future.

Copyright infringement is usually alleged on two grounds:

- AI models sometimes reproduce verbatim content.
- AI providers use copyrighted data without authorization to train models.

Verbatim reproductions happen when a model memorizes training data, which is a result of overfitting. It is likely that AI providers will try to minimize this by using techniques to prevent overfitting. It's hard to guarantee that no memorization will happen, but it might be mitigated successfully.

The second point—that data is used to train models without authorization—is more controversial and seems to be the crux of the problem. Supporters of AI providers argue that it isn't a copyright violation. They think it is legitimate to scrape data to train a model because the goal is for the model to learn patterns and associations from data, not to reproduce a verbatim copy of the data (even if that has happened in some unfortunate cases).

I've even heard some people argue that us humans learn from reading publicly available data, and we then use that knowledge to create our own work. So, why wouldn't AI providers be able to do the same?

The key to this conundrum hinges on the topic of *fair use*. In copyright law, it is considered that copying data without authorization is fair in some circumstances. This includes copying the data to help build a product that does not replace or compete against the original product. For example, throughout this book, I have reproduced quotations from other books. I never reached out to their authors to ask for permission. This

150   *The fine print*

is considered fair use because my quotations don't make this book compete against the other books, and the original author of the quotation is clearly attributed. In chapter 1, for instance, I quoted a paragraph from the book *The Elements of Statistical Learning*. However, this book covers a different topic, so it doesn't intend to compete with it, stealing some of its customers. In fact, I may actually drive some publicity toward that book by mentioning it. Had I copied an entire chapter of that book, however, this wouldn't be considered fair use because my book could become a replacement for it. There are no exact guidelines on what constitutes fair use, such as a precise number of words in a quotation, so this is usually determined case by case in a dispute resolution.

The lawsuits by Getty Images and *The New York Times* attempted to establish that scraping their data by AI providers was not fair use because they used it to build competing products. This allegation is particularly easy to visualize in the case of image generation—one can imagine that customers of Getty Images may use Stable Diffusion instead to create images.

As Getty Images argues (https://mng.bz/RVgO),

> *Stability AI has copied at least 12 million copyrighted images from Getty Images' websites. . . . Stability AI now competes directly with Getty Images.*

The New York Times lawsuit also tries to establish that OpenAI's models act as a replacement to the newspaper's website (https://mng.bz/2yvm):

> *Defendants insist that their conduct is protected as "fair use" because their unlicensed use of copyrighted content to train GenAI models serves a new "transformative" purpose. But there is nothing "transformative" about using The Times's content without payment to create products that substitute for The Times and steal audiences away from it.*

As of this writing, these disputes haven't been settled. We'll see what happens in court.

I think one likely outcome from successive disputes is that regulators will request AI providers to honor opt-out

Economics of AI   151

requests—if a data owner doesn't want their data used to train AI models, it shouldn't be used. The data owner will have to indicate their wish to opt out through machine-readable metadata in an agreed format. This is how it works if you don't want search engines to scrape and index your content. You must specify so in a text file called robots.txt, returned upon request to your root domain (e.g., example.com/robots.txt). In a special format, the file describes which sections of the website are allowed to be scraped and by whom. All major search engines honor the protocol.

A different controversy is whether AI-generated content is itself protected by copyright law. For example, if you generate an image using Midjourney, can you prevent others from reproducing the AI-generated image, as it's a violation of *your* copyright? The Copyright Alliance argues that work solely generated by AI is not protected by copyright. However, it clarifies (https://mng.bz/1Xnn):

> *If a work contains both AI-generated elements and elements of human authorship protectable by copyright law—such as human-authored text or a human's minimally creative arrangement, selection, and coordination of various parts of the work—the elements of the work that are protected by copyright would be owned by the human author.*

I'm not quite sure what this means. If I use Midjourney to generate an image, is the work solely generated by AI, or am I the work's coordinator because I wrote and refined the prompt? Perhaps the Copyright Alliance doesn't know yet, as it adds after that paragraph, "AI and copyright issues will continue to develop," and it invites you to sign up for the newsletter on AI copyright to stay up to date.

Economics of AI

Since the boom of generative AI, we hear a lot about its potential economic rewards. By the sounds of it, a lot of people will make a lot of money thanks to AI. But is that so?

152 *The fine print*

Some AI providers are already collecting billions in revenue. In 2024, for example, OpenAI generated $3.7 billion. This is quite impressive for such a young company.

But revenue is not enough to build a successful business in the long run. For that, a business must become profitable—it must collect more revenue than it spends on generating it. Otherwise, it can't pay the bills unless there's a continued injection of cash from investors to subsidize its losses.

In 2024, OpenAI *lost* $5 billion. While its $3.7-billion revenue was impressive, it wasn't enough to cover its even more impressive expenses (https://mng.bz/PdMv). This was likely related to the high costs of training and serving large AI models. Some people have estimated that running ChatGPT might cost OpenAI $700,000 a day (https://mng.bz/JYna). Training GPT-4 is said to have cost the company $100 million (https://mng.bz/wJma). Note that some models are retrained periodically with new data, so model training is not always a one-off expense. The other major AI providers, such as Anthropic and Mistral, are also still unprofitable.

In addition to becoming profitable, a business is successful if it generates *good* profits—investors want good bang for their buck. In a competitive market, profits tend be eroded over time because copycats enter the market, pushing costs up and prices down, so it's hard to make consistently good profits. The latter requires a *moat*, also known as a *competitive advantage*, which is a feature that protects a company's market share from competitors. When a business benefits from a moat, competitors can't enter the market on equal terms, so it's hard or too expensive for them to eat into your market share.

AI providers don't seem to have a strong moat protecting their market shares. In particular, the methodology behind LLMs (the transformer architecture discussed in chapter 1) is publicly known, so others can build their own competing models. AI providers are a bit uneasy about this. In May 2023, a leaked Google memo said, "We have no moat and neither does OpenAI. . . . The uncomfortable truth is, we aren't positioned to win this arms race and neither is OpenAI. . . .While our AI still holds a slight edge in terms of quality, the gap is closing astonishingly quickly. Open-source AI is faster, more customizable, more private, and pound-for-pound more capable." The memo also admitted, "We have no secret sauce," and it suggested, "People will not pay for restricted AI when free, unrestricted alternatives are comparable in quality. We should consider where our value add really is" (Emmanuel Maggiori, 2024, *Siliconned*).

Because there's no secret sauce, the models created by different providers are already converging in terms of performance and capabilities, including open source ones. It is conceivable that there will be a market shake-up at some point—some companies may go out of business or discontinue their products. The economic case for developing large AI models is not as clear as it may seem initially.

In addition to the big players, numerous smaller companies are building AI-based products, which are built on top of foundation models—some people call them "AI wrappers." For example, there are tens of companies that offer an AI tool to turn an ordinary picture of you into a professional-looking headshot. These tools are likely a thin layer added on top of a publicly available AI model such as Stable Diffusion, or perhaps a fine-tuned version of one of them. This might seem like a winning business idea at first because you're genuinely making it easy to create headshots for people. However, there is no moat—the "secret sauce" of these apps is the prompt which, unless it's very special, others will probably be able to come up with too. So, competition multiplies, as we can already see from the multiple apps offering similar functionality. It will be hard for these thin businesses to generate significant profits.

Finally, much has been said about a dramatic increase in business productivity thanks to the use of AI tools. In 2023, McKinsey shared the following estimates (https://mng.bz/qxz6):

> *Generative AI's impact on productivity could add trillions of dollars in value to the global economy. Our latest research estimates that*

154 *The fine print*

generative AI could add the equivalent of $2.6 trillion to $4.4 trillion annually across the 63 use cases we analyzed—by comparison, the United Kingdom's entire GDP in 2021 was $3.1 trillion.

But productivity increases have been pretty much undetectable so far. A 2024 *Economist* article explains:

Macroeconomic data . . . show little evidence of a surge in productivity . . . In America, the global centre of AI, output per hour remains below its pre-2020 trend. Even in global data derived from surveys of purchasing managers, which are produced with a shorter lag, there is no sign of a productivity surge. ("What happened to the artificial-intelligence revolution?" 2024, July 2, The Economist)

The article also explains that the rate of adoption of AI in the business world has been very slow due to "concerns about data security, biased algorithms and hallucinations." It concludes, "So far the technology has had almost no economic impact." Indeed, it seems that implementing AI in business is harder than it may initially seem. Someone recently told me that the problem was the "last mile"—while AI can help you do the initial 80% of a job just fine, it's hard to make it complete the remaining 20% well because of hallucinations or the need for painstaking customization. This makes productivity gains less impressive than promised.

So, I advise you to be cautious when you hear big statements about AI's economic benefits. The jury is still out.

Smoke and mirrors

In November 2023, it was revealed that self-driving cars produced by Cruise weren't quite driving themselves. An army of human operators in a remote-control room manually intervened when the cars faced problems. This happened once every 2.5 to 5 miles of driving. The company had 1.5 employees doing this job for every car on the streets (https://mng .bz/7pM7). Business professor Thomas W. Malone said, "It may be cheaper just to pay a driver to sit in the car and drive it" (https://mng.bz/mGpW).

Smoke and mirrors   **155**

A few months later, Waymo, which is Cruise's main competitor, explained in a blog article, "Much like phone-a-friend, when the Waymo vehicle encounters a particular situation on the road, the autonomous driver can reach out to a human fleet response agent for additional information to contextualize its environment" (https://waymo.com/blog/2024/05/fleet-response/).

Something similar happened with Amazon's "just walk out" technology, installed in Amazon's supermarkets. This technology allegedly used AI to automatically prepare your shopping receipt based on footage from cameras installed on the ceiling. In April 2024, a reporter revealed that 1,000 remote workers in India were watching the videos and manually preparing or adjusting at least 70% of receipts (https://mng.bz/5gX8).

The use of humans to secretly power AI is often compared to the Mechanical Turk, a fraudulent machine constructed in 1770, which seemed to play chess by itself when, in reality, a human secretly powered it. The machine was exhibited on tours for 84 years.

The AI field is plagued with big promises, hype, and exaggeration. Mechanical Turks are just one example of this—exaggeration and deception come in different forms. In April 2023, for example, Google executives claimed that one of their AI models had learned the Bengali language even though it hadn't been trained on Bengali-language text. One of them explained, "We discovered that with very few amounts of prompting in Bengali, it can now translate all of Bengali" (https://futurism.com/the-byte/google-ai-bengali). They argued that this was an example of AI having "emergent properties."

The news went viral. An Indian newspaper pondered, "AI learns Bengali on its own, should we be worried?" (https://mng.bz/6eyp). Someone who heard about this news reached out to me asking if I thought we might soon face a "singularity event"—a dramatic explosion of AI's capabilities—since now AI could learn new stuff on its own.

156   *The fine print*

With an understanding of how current AI works (see chapter 1), it's hard to believe it could easily learn a new language that is not part of its training data. As it turns out, Bengali was indeed one of the languages the model was trained on, contrary to what the Google executives had said (https://mng.bz/oKYy).

More recently, in September 2024, OpenAI launched a new model called OpenAI o1. The company framed it as a model capable of "thinking" and "reasoning." The announcement explained, "We are introducing OpenAI o1, a new large language model trained with reinforcement learning to perform complex reasoning. o1 thinks before it answers—it can produce a long internal chain of thought before responding to the user" (https://mng.bz/nROV). The article used the word "think" 9 times and the word "reason" 17 times. This framing made it sound like a major improvement and perhaps a departure from the usual autocompleting LLMs. It also sounded like a step toward more human-like AI—the announcement said the model could spend more time thinking before responding, "much like a person would."

But once we look beyond the marketing material, we realize that the o1 system isn't as novel as it seems. It works as follows: first, an LLM is used to generate a piece of text with a suggested list of steps to solve the problem. These instructions are then added to the end of the original prompt. So, the new prompt contains the original task followed by a suggested step-by-step recipe to perform it. Afterward, this extended prompt is run through an LLM as usual. This mimics the popular chain-of-thought prompting technique, in which the user adds a step-by-step guideline of how to solve a problem to the prompt.

The announcement emphasized that reinforcement learning was used to train the system: "Our large-scale reinforcement learning algorithm teaches the model how to think productively using its chain of thought in a highly data-efficient training process." This may sound impressive, but it's probably

Regulation

nothing new. OpenAI has been using reinforcement learning with human feedback (RLHF) to refine all its models for quite some time (see chapter 1). It's likely that by "reinforcement learning" they meant that humans manually wrote down a small dataset of examples of the step-by-step instructions they wanted the LLM to generate, and the LLM was refined to produce such instructions more accurately.

I advise you to be cautious whenever you hear impressive AI announcements. I recommend keeping in mind how current AI works when you analyze announcements, which makes it easier to read between the lines and separate the wheat from the chaff.

Regulation

In August 2024, regulation concerning AI came into force in the European Union, known as the AI Act. The AI Act applies to AI that is used, or whose outputs are used, inside the EU, even if it's developed and run elsewhere. The regulation has been controversial, with some people deeming it insufficient and others excessive. Either way, let's have a quick discussion about it because you might be affected (e.g., you might develop an AI-based product used in the EU) and because it may become the blueprint for future AI regulation elsewhere.

The AI Act contains four special chapters that are especially relevant to developers and users of AI systems. We briefly comment on each of them below. You can read the full text online (https://mng.bz/vKWm) or have a look at the official high-level summary (https://mng.bz/4aQ5).

Prohibited AI practices

This part of the Act describes a list of AI practices that are outright prohibited as they're considered serious violations. These include AI used to manipulate or deceive people, AI that exploits people's vulnerabilities "due to their age, disability or a specific social or economic situation," and AI for social scoring, among other categories.

High-risk systems

This part contains stipulations that apply to high-risk products. These are products that are already regulated by the EU and require a third-party conformity assessment, such as certain vehicles, machinery, and medical devices. It also adds a few more categories to the list, such as AI for targeted job ads and AI for visa applications. The Act imposes several requirements on these high-risk systems, including enabling human oversight "to understand its capabilities and limitations, detect and address issues, avoid over-reliance on the system, interpret its output, decide not to use it, or stop its operation."

Transparency obligations

This part requires companies to inform users when they're interacting with an AI system ("unless it's obvious or the AI is used for legal purposes like crime detection"), which specifically applies to "an AI system that generates or manipulates image, audio or video content constituting a deep fake." This is the case even with systems that are not deemed high risk. Note that if you use AI to generate content but then you thoroughly review the content and hold editorial responsibility over it, you no longer need to inform others about using AI.

By the way, don't worry about the AI Act ruining your AI art—you can indicate that you're using AI "in an appropriate manner that does not hamper the display or enjoyment of the work."

Foundation models

This part imposes requirements on foundation models, which are denoted by "general-purpose AI models." The Act requires the AI provider to write documentation detailing the model's development, including "information on the data used for training, testing and validation" and "known or estimated energy consumption of the model."

In addition, there's a special category of very large foundation models the Act deems to pose "systemic risk." These are models that exceed a certain threshold in terms of the amount of training (the threshold is currently set to 10^{25} floating-point operations during training). The creators of these models must notify the EU of their work, and the EU might impose additional requirements to mitigate risk.

In addition, the Act approves training models from scraped data without authorization, so long as opt-outs are respected. This was approved indirectly by referring the reader to a directive that allows web scraping with the goal of data mining for analytics purposes. Some people have criticized this directive saying that "data mining" is too broad and could cover pretty much anything (https://mng.bz/QDa1).

Resource consumption

Training and using AI models consumes electricity and other resources, the scale of which has been criticized. For example, a journalist called AI "a disaster for the climate" (https://mng.bz/Xxzl).

It is difficult to gauge AI's electricity consumption because providers haven't yet reported it consistently. So, we have to rely on studies made by other people. These studies aren't quite standardized, so they're a bit messy and difficult to follow. Some of them even mix different units within the same report in a chaotic way, such as kWh, CO2 emissions, and "equivalent number of smartphone charges" (https://arxiv.org/pdf/2311.16863). Sometimes researchers rely on hearsay and loose logical connections to calculate consumption. For example, one researcher deduced LLMs' energy consumption indirectly from the fact that a Google executive said in an interview that LLMs likely consumed 10 times more power than performing a Google search (https://mng.bz/yW57).

In the following, I'll share some results from a study presented by a group of researchers from Hugging Face and Carnegie Mellon University. The researchers used multiple open source models with their own GPUs and measured consumption.

160   *The fine print*

Table 6.1 shows electricity consumption reported by the researchers for text and image generation (https://arxiv.org/pdf/2311.16863). Consumption figures are the average across different models studied by the researchers (individual consumption per model was not reported in a consistent manner).

Table 6.1   Average electricity consumption across different models compared with typical household consumption

	kWh / 1,000 responses	% of daily household kWh (US)	% of daily household kWh (UK)
Text generation	0.047	0.15%	0.5%
Image generation	2.907	9.83%	30%

Note that the figures are per 1,000 uses of the model, such as generating an entire response 1,000 times with an LLM or generating 1,000 images with a text-to-image model. One thousand uses of AI may seem like a lot, but it might easily be reached by intensive users in less than a day. For example, a coder using GitHub Copilot might generate hundreds of LLM-based autocompletions every hour. Moreover, many of our regular online actions, such as performing a Google search or browsing an online store, may trigger LLM queries (Google is already showing AI results with searches), which would add more LLM usage even if the user doesn't use LLMs directly. We can also imagine that a small group of graphic designers might generate 1,000 images in a short time frame by prompting the system repeatedly to create images and adjust the result.

In these experiments, image generation was much more power-hungry than text generation. However, the researchers didn't reveal the prompt used for text generation or how much text was generated each time. In addition, they only used text-generation models on the smaller end of the spectrum, such as GPT-2 models, which are 100 times smaller than the generation that succeeded them. The authors reported

Resource consumption

significant variability across models. In particular, the largest image-generation model consumed 6,000 times as much power as the smallest one.

Note that AI models are constantly being optimized, so consumption could be reduced in the future—sometimes a model can be made much smaller without significantly reducing its capabilities. For reference, I've added two columns to table 6.1 that compare AI consumption with the total daily electricity consumption by the typical US (https://www.eia.gov/tools/faqs/faq.php?id=97&t=3) and UK (https://mng.bz/MDQE) households.

The greatest worry is not electricity consumption itself, but the CO_2 emitted to generate it. *Carbon intensity* measures the grams of CO_2 emitted per kWh consumed, and it varies depending on how power is generated. Table 6.2 restates the above results in terms of CO_2 emitted based on typical carbon intensity in the US (https://mng.bz/av6x) and the UK (https://mng.bz/gaXZ; both countries produce electricity from different sources, so their carbon intensity differs).

Table 6.2   Comparison of the electricity consumption from table 6.1 with equivalent CO_2 emissions of petrol cars

	Grams of CO_2 / 1,000 responses (US)	Miles driven for equivalent CO_2 (US)	Grams of CO_2 / 1,000 responses (UK)	Miles driven for equivalent CO_2 (UK)
Text generation	20	0.05 miles	7.6	0.02 miles
Image generation	1,200	3.1 miles	470	1.2 miles

To put things in perspective, the table includes the number of miles you'd have to drive a car to emit the same amount of CO2 (https://mng.bz/av6x).

In addition to the electricity required to use AI models, many people have stressed that *training* them is a power-hungry

162   *The fine print*

activity. It's been estimated that training GPT-3 consumed 1,287 MWh (https://arxiv.org/pdf/2104.10350). This amounted to the electricity consumed in one day by 43,000 US households or 134,000 UK households. Note that, while models are only trained sporadically, AI providers train or retrain multiple models a year.

Using and training AI models also consumes other resources, such as water for cooling down data centers. An article in *Fortune* explained, "Microsoft disclosed that its global water consumption spiked 34% from 2021 to 2022 (to nearly 1.7 billion gallons, or more than 2,500 Olympic-sized swimming pools), a sharp increase compared to previous years that outside researchers tie to its AI research" (https://mng.bz/eyNw).

When you use AI, I recommend you keep in mind that "cloud computing" actually happens on Earth, inside large refrigerated buildings, and this can be resource-intensive and have an influence on the environment.

Brains and consciousness

Let's finish on a lighter and more philosophical note. It is common to compare the structure of AI models with our own biological brains. If you remember from chapter 1, LLMs perform lots of projections, which are mathematical operations that involve matrix multiplications. Biological neurons have been traditionally described as performing a similar calculation, so many ML models, including LLMs, are categorized as *artificial neural networks*. In addition, some ML model architectures have been compared with the structure of specific parts of our brains. For example, convolutional neural networks (CNNs) are often compared with the brain's visual cortex.

In reality, we still don't quite understand how brains work. For example, the traditional understanding of the calculations made by neurons is too simple (Penrose, R., 1989, *The Emperor's New Mind: Concerning Computers, Mind, and the Laws in Physics.* Oxford University Press, p. 511). Over the years,

Brains and consciousness

163

much more complicated models have been developed. However, these models still cannot predict what scientists observe when studying the workings of real neurons. For example, in 2020, a group of researchers discovered that the dendrites that pass signals from one neuron to another may actually carry out complicated computations (Gidon, A. et al., 2020, "Dendritic action potentials and computation in human layer 2/3 cortical neurons," *Science, 367*[6473], pp. 83–87). So, they aren't just wires that carry signals as previously thought. To complicate things even more, the fluid that surrounds neurons contains molecules, known as neuromodulators, which affect neurons' behavior in a way that isn't fully understood. While progress has been made, our understanding of neurons and brains is still quite poor.

As of today, the brain of only one organism has been fully mapped out, meaning that researchers could create a map of all connections between neurons, or *connectome*. The organism is a tiny worm called C. Elegans, which has around 300 neurons and 7,000 connections among them. However, it was impossible to simulate the observed worm's behavior, as the map just tells us which neurons are connected to which but not exactly how they work. Neuroscientist Anthony Movshon concluded that the "connectome by itself has not explained anything" (Jabr, F., 2012, "The Connectome Debate: Is Mapping the Mind of a Worm Worth It?" *Scientific American,* https://mng.bz/pKaE).

In some cases, AI models are designed without considering brain structures, and the brain analogy is forced later on. For example, the initial articles describing CNNs did *not* say that these were inspired by the brain. The researchers claimed their design decisions were "guided by our prior knowledge about shape recognition" (LeCun, Y. et al., 1989, "Handwritten digit recognition with a back-propagation network," *Advances in Neural Information Processing Systems,* 2). Years later, when CNNs became popular, the same researchers claimed that they were "directly inspired by the classic notions of simple cells and complex cells in visual neuroscience, and the overall architecture is

164 *The fine print*

reminiscent of the LGN–V1–V2–V4–IT hierarchy in the visual cortex ventral pathway" (LeCun, Y., Bengio, Y., & Hinton, G., 2015, "Deep learning," *Nature, 521*[7553], pp. 436–444).

Moreover, analogies are often quite loose. For example, the comparison between CNNs and the visual cortex only works if we ignore some known things about the visual cortex that are not a part of CNNs (see *Smart Until It's Dumb*, Chapter 2).

So, be cautious whenever you hear analogies between AI and brains. We still don't understand brains, so the connection is likely to be highly speculative.

In addition to brain-related speculation, the latest AI boom has also reignited the consciousness debate. Just to cite an example, in 2022, the news went viral that an AI engineer claimed Google's chatbot had become sentient (https://mng.bz/OBn2).

But, just like with brains, we don't quite understand consciousness. We do know that some parts of the brain are in charge of unconscious actions (like controlling heartbeat), while others are related to conscious perceptions (like vision), but we don't understand why some parts contribute to our consciousness, while others don't. We also don't understand how general anesthesia works; we just know from experience that anesthetics turn off consciousness temporarily, but we don't know the mechanism behind it.

In addition, there are many philosophical questions around consciousness that don't have an easy answer. For example, some people think that any computation gives rise to consciousness. Under this view, a thermostat is conscious but in a different way. Other people, like physicist Roger Penrose, think consciousness doesn't arise from computation at all and thus cannot be created with digital computers. The debate is still ongoing, and I'm not sure we'll ever be able to determine whether a thermostat is conscious.

So, I advise you to be cautious when anyone claims to have a definitive answer about the link between AI and consciousness. There is so much we don't know.

As we've now reached the end of this book, let's quickly reflect on the content covered. Throughout this book, we've discussed the power of AI—how ML innovations have pushed the boundaries of what AI can do. We've also discussed AI's limitations—how sometimes AI hallucinates or isn't as useful as it seems at first sight. Because AI is not all-powerful, its effects will vary depending on the context—sometimes AI may automate away jobs, but other times it may not; sometimes it may be the best tool for a task, but other times it may not; and so on. In this book, I tried to cover both sides of that debate and share advice accordingly. The last chapter completed our analysis by discussing some of the bigger questions surrounding AI, many of which are still unanswered and are likely to be hot topics in the future.

Summary

- The copyright debate hinges on the interpretation of *fair use*. AI providers argue that they scrape data so that their models can learn general patterns and that they don't intend to reproduce the original data, implying it's a fair use of that data. Data owners argue that AI providers use this data to build competing products and steal their customers, so this isn't fair use.

- The economic case for AI is not that clear. AI providers are still largely unprofitable and face fierce competition. Smaller companies that create thin AI wrappers also face fierce competition and may struggle to make ends meet. Productivity gains in the wider economy due to AI have not yet been observed.

- The AI field has a tendency to exaggerate or even deceive. Many products that allegedly used AI have been revealed to rely on remote human operators to do the job manually. Big AI announcements are often incorrect (like Google saying a model learned a language that wasn't in its training data) or spruced up (like OpenAI saying its model "thinks" and "reasons").

- The amount of electricity consumption (and other resources like water) to train and run AI models has received a lot of criticism, with some people arguing it will have detrimental environmental effects. Studies and reports about AI resource consumption are still scarce and preliminary, but we can see that it isn't a negligible amount.

- Comparisons between AI models and the structure of the brain are highly speculative. We don't quite understand how brains work yet, so comparisons tend to be forced. The same goes for AI and consciousness—it's still an ongoing debate without clear-cut answers.

appendix A
Catalog of
generative AI tools

This appendix lists many popular generative AI tools available at the time of writing. I expect some parts of the AI market to organize as an oligopoly, meaning that there will be a few key players instead of a multitude. This will be especially true of companies that build foundation models, as model training incurs high one-off costs that few companies will be able to afford. So, the market of foundation models will become similar to the cloud computing market, which is dominated by three main competitors.

Furthermore, I expect convergence in terms of models' capabilities, as different foundation models are becoming increasingly similar. There also seems to be a tendency toward building multimodal AI, so you may not need to use different models to process text, images, and video.

In other cases, such as lighter AI apps (e.g., simple wrappers around LLMs) or smaller specialized AI models, we may observe a multitude of competitors. This market may become similar to fitness apps, in which there are thousands of options to choose from.

168   **APPENDIX A**   *Catalog of generative AI tools*

General-purpose conversational AI

Let's first have a look at the market for general-purpose AI chatbots, categorized into customer-facing apps, proprietary foundation models, and open source foundation models.

Customer-facing apps

- *ChatGPT*—An AI assistant developed by OpenAI. It operates on a freemium basis (free access to some functionality and a monthly subscription to access additional features). It can be accessed at https://chatgpt.com.

- *Claude*—An AI assistant developed by Anthropic, an AI company launched by former OpenAI employees. It operates on a freemium basis and can be accessed at https://claude.ai.

- *Gemini*—An AI assistant developed by Google via its subsidiary Google DeepMind. It operates on a freemium basis and can be accessed at https://gemini.google.com.

- *Microsoft Copilot*—An AI assistant developed by Microsoft. It operates on a freemium basis and can be accessed through various Microsoft apps, such as Word and Excel, as well as directly through the browser at https://copilot.microsoft.com. It's also possible to access Copilot directly from the Windows 11 taskbar, and some PCs are already being manufactured with a dedicated Copilot key in their keyboards.

- *Perplexity AI*—A freemium AI chatbot meant to be used as a search engine. It relies on various foundation models under the hood, including some manufactured by other companies like OpenAI and Anthropic. It can be used at https://perplexity.ai.

Foundation models (proprietary)

- *GPT*—A family of general-purpose, multimodal models developed by OpenAI, which includes GPT-4 and GPT-4o.

They can be accessed through the OpenAI API. Some of these models power customer-facing ChatGPT.

- *Gemini*—A family of general-purpose, multimodal models developed by Google, which includes Gemini 1.5 Flash and Gemini 1.5 Pro, the former being faster but less capable than its Pro variant. Gemini models power Google's customer-facing Gemini.

- *Claude*—A family of general-purpose, multimodal models developed by Anthropic, which includes Claude Haiku, Claude Sonnet, and Claude Opus (in increasing order of complexity). They can be accessed through the Anthropic API. Some of these models power customer-facing Claude.

Foundation models (open source)

- *Llama*—A family of general-purpose, multimodal models developed by Meta. The model architecture and its parameters are publicly available, but training data has not been disclosed. These models are released under a special-purpose license called Meta Llama Community License, which imposes some usage restrictions.

- *DeepSeek*—A family of models developed by the Chinese AI company DeepSeek. Its most prominent model, Deep-Seek-V3, made headlines for being as performing but much cheaper to train than competitors, which caused Nvidia's stock to crash. The code to run the model is publicly available, but training code and training data haven't been disclosed. Its license is permissive but imposes some usage restrictions.

- *Mistral*—A family of models developed by French company Mistral AI, which was founded to become the European contender to OpenAI. The company publishes text-only models (e.g., Mistral Large 2) and vision-capable models (e.g., Pixtral 12B). They're released under the highly permissive Apache 2.0 license, but the training data has not been disclosed.

170   **APPENDIX A**   *Catalog of generative AI tools*

- *Gemma*—A family of general-purpose models developed by Google as an open source counterpart to its proprietary Gemini models. Some models are text-only (e.g., Gemma 2), while others can handle input images (e.g., PaliGemma). The models are released under the permissive Apache 2.0 license, but the training data has not been disclosed.

- *Phi*—A family of lightweight general-purpose language models developed by Microsoft, including Phi-3 Mini and Phi-3 Medium. They're released under the permissive MIT License, but the training data has not been disclosed.

Coding assistants

The following are popular tools that help software engineers write code:

- *GitHub Copilot*—An AI coding assistant that can be installed as a plug-in on multiple popular IDEs. It can be used mainly in two different ways. One way is to type into a chat window to interact with a chatbot and ask questions about the code or ask it to perform tasks. The other way is for the assistant to autocomplete your code as you type it—you can accept suggestions by pressing the Tab key on your keyboard. You must pay a monthly subscription to use it, but there is a free trial.

- *Cursor*—A standalone, AI-powered IDE, built on top of Visual Studio. You can chat with the AI assistant or accept code autocompletions by pressing the Tab key. There is a free version with a limited number of completions and paid subscriptions with a higher number or an unlimited number of completions.

- *JetBrains AI Pro*—The company behind popular IDEs such as PyCharm and IntelliJ offers an add-on subscription to access an AI assistant. You can chat with the assistant about the code, and you can also accept autocompletions by pressing the Tab key. These autocompletions are powered by their cloud-based LLM, but users not subscribed to the AI add-on can still benefit from simpler autocompletions run locally. Users must pay a monthly license to add the AI assistant to its IDEs.

Image generation

We now discuss AI for image generation, categorized into customer-facing apps, proprietary foundation models, and open source foundation models.

Customer-facing apps

- *Midjourney*—A tool to generate images from a textual description (and optionally reference images to influence the output). The app is used directly on Midjourney's website (https://midjourney.com) or through a Discord chat. The app initially generates four different image variants of size 1024 × 1024 each. You can then pick your favorite one, refine it, and increase its size (or upscale it). You must pay a monthly fee to access Midjourney, with different plans imposing different usage limits.

- *Dall-E*—OpenAI's flagship text-to-image app. It has now been integrated into ChatGPT, so it can be used directly by asking ChatGPT to produce images (although OpenAI still offers a dedicated DALL-E interface on https://chatpgt.com). Only paid OpenAI subscribers can access it.

Foundation models (proprietary)

- *Dall-E*—OpenAI provides API access to its image-generation models. Users pay per image generated, with prices varying according to the model's version and image size.

- *Flux.1 Pro*—A text-to-image model developed by Black Forest Labs, which has been praised for its photorealism. It can be accessed through various APIs from providers

172   **APPENDIX A**   *Catalog of generative AI tools*

that have partnered up with Black Forest Labs, which include Replicate and Together AI.

Foundation models (open source)

- *Stable Diffusion*—A family of text-to-image models developed by Stability AI, built using a diffusion approach (see chapter 1). In addition to making the models publicly available, the company has released the data used to train its models and the algorithms used to filter and curate the data. Stable Diffusion is released under an open source license with usage restrictions. In particular, users are not allowed to "generate or disseminate verifiably false information," "harm minors," or "provide medical advice," among other restrictions (https://mng.bz/YDpe).

- *Flux.1 Schnell and Flux.1 Dev*—These models, derived from proprietary Flux.1 Pro, have been made open source by Black Forest Labs. Flux.1 Schnell has been released under the permissive Apache 2.0 license. The more powerful but slower Flux.1 Dev has been released under a license that forbids commercial use. Training data has not been made publicly available.

DIY

We finish with some of the tools and libraries commonly used to fine-tune or create your own AI models:

- *Hugging Face*—This company hosts the de facto repository of AI models. Open source models are usually published there. The company also maintains a suite of libraries, including *Transformers,* which helps use pretrained models. The company also maintains libraries that help fine-tune models easily.

- *PyTorch*—A popular Python library used to create and train machine learning models. Historically, PyTorch has been favored by the academic community, which uses the

DIY

library to quickly prototype and analyze models, although it seems to be growing in popularity elsewhere. Hugging Face's Transformers library is built on top of PyTorch.

- *TensorFlow*—A popular alternative to PyTorch. It is usually favored by those who deploy high-performing ML models in production, although it seems to be losing popularity to PyTorch as of late. The GPT-2 model, whose code was made publicly available by OpenAI, uses TensorFlow (https://github.com/openai/gpt-2/). OpenAI has switched to PyTorch as its preferred library since then (https://openai.com/index/openai-pytorch/).

index

A

accuracy 93
AI (artificial intelligence) 1
  brains and consciousness 162–165
  building AI-based product 99–104
  controversies and discussions 146
  conversational AI 105–111
  convolutions 51–53
  copyright 147–151
  economics of 151–154
  embeddings 19–24
  impact on jobs, making web more
    human 141
  LLM wrappers 113–114
  (ML) machine learning 36–50,
    53–56
  multimodal AI 53–56
  performance measures 93–96
  selecting and evaluating tools 82
  self-driving cars 154–157
  tight control 136–141
  tokens 13–18
  transformer architecture 25–35
  validation 126–136
  when to use 98
AI tools
  customer-facing AI apps vs.
    foundation models 89

off-the-shelf vs. fine-tuning 86–89
Amazon 155
artificial neural networks 162
attention mechanism 29
automation, mass unemployment
    and 142–144
autoregressive 3

B

batches 49
billing by tokens 16
Boto3 library 107
brains and consciousness 162–165
byte pair encoding 14

C

carbon intensity 161
chain-of-thought prompting 76, 156
chat 5
CNNs (convolutional neural
    networks) 68, 162
competitive advantage 124, 152
completions mode 6
conditional diffusion model 54
connectome, defined 163
contextualization 29–32
  multiheaded attention 32
  multilayer architecture 31
context window 27

176 INDEX

conversational AI 105–111
  describing task and validating
    output 106
  excellent job 110
  previous work 107–110
convolutions 51–53
copyright 147–151
cross-entropy loss 48
customer-facing AI apps 89

D

datasets 90
deep learning 37
dimension 19
discriminative model 51
dot product 22
dropout 87

E

early stopping 87
embeddings 19–24
  initial 28
  LLMs and struggles with analyzing
    individual letters 24
  machine learning and 20
  usefulness of 22
  visualizing 21
end of text 5
epochs 50
excellence gap 118–126
  in software engineering 122–124
exploitation 42
exploration 42
external software functions 8

F

fair use 150
feature flag 135
few-shot prompting 86
fine-tuning 47, 86
foundation models 89, 158

G

generative AI 51
get_current_weather function 10, 12
Google Places API 114
GPT-2 45
GraphHopper 106

H

hallucinations 59–67
  causes of 68–74
  impact on products 78–80
  incorrect solutions to problems
    63–65
  living with 80
  made-up facts 61
  misinterpretation 62
  mitigation 75–78
  overconfidence 65
  unpredictability 66
Hazlitt, Henry 143

I

Illustrated Transformer, The (book) 35
inference time 50
input prompts, subdividing into valid
  tokens 14
InstructGPT 46

J

jobs 117

L

languages, other than English 16
learnable parameters 28
limited scope of updates 87
LLMs (large language models) 2–13
  calling external software
    functions 8
  chat 5
  end of text 5
  hallucinations, will they go
    away? 74
  need for tokens 18
  retrieval-augmented generation 12

INDEX

struggles with analyzing individual
letters 24
system prompt 7
text generation 4
training 45–47
wrapper 3, 113–114
local minimum 50
loss 48
LSTM (long short-term memory) 25

M

made-up facts 61
MAE (mean absolute error) 96, 97
Maggiori, Emmanuel 60
mass unemployment 142–144
Mechanical Turk 155
minibatches 49
misaligned objectives 70
misinterpretation 62
ML (machine learning) 2, 36–50
architecture 56
deep learning 37
embeddings 20
loss 48
stochastic gradient descent 48–50
training LLMs 45–47
types of 38–45
reinforcement learning 42
self-supervised learning 41
simulated data 40
supervised learning 38
unsupervised learning 43
moat 152
model validation, selection, and
testing 90–93
test set 92
training set 90
validation set 91
multiagent AI 78
multiheaded attention 32
multilayer architecture 31
multimodal AI 53–56

MVP (minimum viable product) 124

N

No Free Lunch Theorem 57
NSA (National Security Agency) 118

O

off-the-shelf vs. fine-tuning 86–89
deciding between 88
OpenAI o1 model 156
open source AI 83–85
deciding between proprietary
and 84
operations research 125
overconfidence 65
overfitting 39, 87

P

parameters (not defined by hand) 36
performance measures 93–96
accuracy 93
MAE 96
precision 94–95
recall 94–95
RMSE 96
predictions 32
price optimization 72
privacy 47
projection 23
prompt engineering 76
prompts 3
proprietary AI 83–85
deciding between proprietary and
open source 84

Q

QA (quality assurance) teams 131

R

RAG (retrieval-augmented
generation) 12, 62, 77
recall, defined 94–95
regularization 87
regulation 157

foundation models 158
high-risk systems 158
prohibited AI practices 157
transparency obligations 158
reinforcement learning 42, 47
reproducible outputs 34
resource consumption 159–162
reward model 43
RLHF (reinforcement learning with human feedback) 43, 76, 157
RL (reinforcement learning) 42
RMSE (root mean squared error) 96, 97

S

self-driving cars 154–157
self-supervised learning 41
SGD (stochastic gradient descent) 48–50
simulated data 40
singularity event 155
SMOTE (synthetic minority oversampling technique) 41
software engineering 122–124
validation in 131–133
solutions to problems, incorrect 63–65
subdividing input prompts into valid tokens 14
supervised learning 38
system prompt 7

T

TDD (test-driven development) 134
temperature 33
Top-k setting 34
Top-p setting 34
test set 92
text generation 4
tight control 136–141
in software 139
recommendations 140
tokens 13–18
billing by 16

languages other than English 16
need for 18
subdividing input prompts into valid tokens 14
tools, AI
deciding between proprietary and open source 84
proprietary vs. open source 83–85
Top-k setting 34
Top-p setting 34
training data 39
training set 90
training time 50
transformer architecture 25–35
contextualization 29–32
initial embeddings 28
learning more about 35
predictions 32
reproducible outputs 34
temperature 33
transparency obligations 158

U

underfitting 39
unpredictability 66
unsupervised learning 43

V

validation 126–136
in software engineering 131–133
recommendations 133–136
validation set 91
visualizing, embeddings 21

W

Waymo 155
world models 68–70

X

XAI (explainable AI) 104

Z

zero-shot prompting 86